The Webmaster's Guide to VB Script

The Webmaster's Guide to VB Script

Jim Keogh

AP PROFESSIONAL

AP PROFESSIONAL is a division of Academic Press, Inc.

Boston San Diego New York
London Sydney Tokyo Toronto

AP PROFESSIONAL
An Imprint of ACADEMIC PRESS, INC.
A Division of HARCOURT BRACE & COMPANY

ORDERS (USA and Canada): 1-800-3131-APP or APP@ACAD.COM
AP Professional Orders: 6277 Sea Harbor Dr., Orlando, FL 32821-9816

Europe/Middle East/Africa: 0-11-44 (0) 181-300-3322
Orders: AP Professional 24–28 Oval Rd., London NW1 7DX

Japan/Korea: 03-3234-3911-5
Orders: Harcourt Brace Japan, Inc., Ichibunan

Australia: 02-517-8999
Orders: Harcourt Brace & Co. Australia, Locked Bag 16, Marrickville, NSW 2204, Australia

Other International: (407) 345-3800
AP Professional Orders: 6277 Sea Harbor Dr., Orlando FL 32821-9816

Editorial: 1300 Boylston St., Chestnut Hill, MA 02167; (617) 232-0500

Web: http://www.apnet.com/

This book is printed on acid-free paper. ♾

United Kingdom Edition published by
ACADEMIC PRESS LIMITED
24–28 Oval Road, London NW1 7DX

Library of Congress Cataloging-in-Publication Data
Keogh, James Edward, 1948–
The Webmaster's guide to VB script / Jim Keogh.
p. cm.
Includes index.
ISBN 0-12-703875-2
1. VBScript (Computer program language) 2. HTML (Document markup language 3. World Wide Web (Information retrieval system)
I. Title.
QA76.73.V27K46 1996
005.2--dc20 96-29307
CIP

Printed in the United States of America
96 97 98 99 CP 9 8 7 6 5 4 3 2 1

Contents

Chapter 1

Enhancing Your Web Page with VB Script

INSIDE THE MYTHICAL WORLD OF CYBERSPACE

From out of cyberspace comes photos, music, and plenty of text on any topic that can be imagined. Once you've been wowed by this magic, no doubt your curiosity will be aroused. At this point you're at a crossroad in cyberspace. You can recognize that cyberspace software developers are whiz kids, then use the fruit of their labor for your own purpose, or you can decide to become one of those whiz kids yourself, then dazzle your friends with your own brand of magic. And, who knows, just maybe you'll be the next Bill Gates.

Well, you're reading this book, so it is safe to say that you want to don those robes and create your own piece of cyberspace. Hold on to your magic carpet. You're about to be taken behind the scenes and taught how to sprinkle a little of your own magic dust to transform your link to cyberspace into a professional Web site that you can call your own.

Let's begin by breaking down some myths. Cyberspace is nothing magic. It is a popular name given to the Internet. The Internet is a network of computers very similar to the computer networks that exist in many businesses. A computer network has three fundamental components: computers, cabling, and software.

At the center of the network is at least one computer called a *server*. A server performs many tasks such as handling calls from other computers, storing information that can be shared with other computers, and even processing information for other computers.

Each computer on the network has an *address*, which is nothing more than a private telephone number that another computer can dial using special network software. Network software is like the network's telephone operator, which answers the call from a computer, then connects the call to another computer.

Does this sound familiar? Don't confuse those computer telephone numbers with telephone numbers that you dial to reach into cyberspace. You don't see this private telephone number unless you dig deep into the bowels of the network software, which is not recommended. Instead, you use an alias for this private telephone number. An alias is like Burt or Ernie, a name we humans can easily relate to. The computer converts these names to the real private telephone number of the other computer.

The Internet has a computer called a server. Actually, the Internet has thousands of servers based all over the world. A server is a high-power computer that stores your Web page and acts like a host to visitors to your Web site by responding to their requests to see more of your Web page. The Internet has other computers—millions of them—just like your computer, and cabling connects all these computers and servers. This is called the *international telephone network*. And, of course, each computer has software that allows the computer to talk electronically to other computers.

What about those telephone numbers? Actually, you use two telephone numbers on the Internet. The first telephone number is the number you dial to link your computer to a service provider's server, which is used as your home base on the Internet. A service provider, usually an organization, has many telephone lines to receive incoming calls like yours.

Outgoing calls are handled by special ISDN lines. An *ISDN line* is a telephone line that is designed to transport many digital signals at lightning speed to other servers on the Internet. The second telephone number is actually the private telephone number of the server that contains the information you want to access.

BEHIND THE SCENES OF YOUR WEB SITE

Now that you have a general view of this mythical world called cyberspace, let's focus on your piece of the action, your Web site. The Internet is a collection of servers owned by any organization that wants to maintain a server site on the Internet. Traditionally, these servers are owned by universities, government agencies, commercial enterprises, clubs, and a few individuals. Anyone who is willing to read a few books on setting up an Internet server and to finance the operation can have his or her own server on the Internet.

Hold on! Don't rush to purchase expensive equipment to make your presence known on the Internet. Save your money and concentrate on building a Web site, not a server site. A subset of the Internet services is called the *World Wide Web*. This segment of the Internet is what most of us consider cyberspace.

The World Wide Web is a loosely organized group of software files that contain specially coded text and graphics. These files are stored on servers connected to the Internet just like you store files in a directory on your hard disk. The directory in which these files are stored on the server is called *public_html*. This directory is technically the Web site.

You can arrange with a service provider to have your own set of directories on the provider's Internet server—your own public_html directory. For a one-time startup fee then a monthly rental fee, you'll receive your own Web site, complete with a private telephone number that has an alias you name. Then anyone can connect to your Web site the same way as to Microsoft or any other site. Someone simply refers to the alias for the Internet private telephone number for your site, like www.microsoft.com.

Of course, establishing your Web site takes a little more effort than simply paying a service provider. Remember, those fees are only for rental space on the Internet server and telephone line usage. You still have to create the files for your Web site. This is called your *Web page*. And that's the reason that you are reading this book. We'll show you how to create the files necessary to run a professional Web site.

EVERYTHING IS IN THE BROWSER

Before we get too far ahead of ourselves, let's complete our behind the scenes tour of the cyberspace magic show. The magic wand of the World Wide Web is software called the *browser*. You're probably familiar with the popular Netscape browser. A variety of browsers are on the market, most given free of charge by service providers to their subscribers.

Why are browsers so important? The browser software determines what you are going to see on the computer screen. The creator of the Web site is totally dependent on the browser used by the millions of computer users he or she hopes will stop by that Web site.

Here's how the browser works. We said that Web sites contain coded text files. A coded text file, referred to as an *HTML file*, contains two kinds of information: text that is to be displayed on the computer and codes that are interpreted by the browser to determine how the text is to be displayed.

Say you want a two-line headline. Each line is to be displayed in a different size type. You can embed special codes preceding each line to ask that the browser display the text in the different size type. Yes, we said *ask*. It is still up to the browser to recognize the code properly, then display the text accordingly. You'll never know if the text is displayed according to your directions unless you test your Web site using the most popular browsers on the market.

All right, that is an overstatement. Most browsers conform to a widely accepted HTML code standard. We'll explore this standard in the next chapter. However, some new additions to the standards are probably not recognized by older browsers. And, of course, some browsers may not adhere to those standards.

After you use software called a *dialer* to connect to your Internet service provider, the browser will be displayed on the computer screen. Next, enter the alias for the Web site that contains information you want to see. The browser looks up the alias in a file and finds the corresponding private telephone number of the Web site server, then dials that number along the Internet.

Once the connection is made, the Web site server and your service provider's server talk to each other then copy the key file of the Web site to your computer. This file is always called *index.html*. The contents of the index.html file are anything you want as long as you conform to the HTML standards.

On most Web sites, the index.html file tells your browser to copy and display a graphic file from the Web site server and then to display text contained in the index.html file. Special text is highlighted on the screen, signaling that if the user points to it and clicks the left mouse button, the browser will load another file from the Web site server or jump to a portion of the current file that is loaded into your computer. This is called *hypertext* (discussed in the next chapter) and it allows the user to quickly move around a Web site.

All the Web site server is doing is copying files to your computer at the request of your browser. Your browser is actually doing all the fancy magical work.

THE BROWSER PUFFED AND PUFFED BUT COULDN'T PERFORM

The job of your Internet browser is to request files from the Web site, then follow the HTML code embedded in the file to make the text come alive on your computer screen. However, if the browser cannot interpret the HTML code properly, you can expect to be disappointed in the Web site no matter how much time and effort the creator has spent building bells and whistles into a Web site file.

Nearly all browsers can understand simple HTML coding, enough so that the browser knows to request a graphic file from the Web site just when a picture is needed on the screen. However, a smart browser realizes that a typical graphic file, such as a bit map, contains thousands of bytes. Each one needs to travel thousands of miles over telephone lines into your computer so that the browser can place the proper pixels on the screen to form the picture.

The smart browser also knows that people are impatient and expect to see these dramatic pictures pop on to their computer screens. However, instant graphics isn't going to happen until many more lanes are opened on the telephone highway. This is technically called *bandwidth*. Simply, the wider the bandwidth, the more bytes can flow faster along cyberspace and into a computer. Fiber-optic cabling offers this facility, and telephone companies are rushing to convert their portion of the superhighway from copper to fiber-optic cabling.

Until cyberspace is retrofitted with this new pavement, we'll have to count on smart browsers to ease the pain of waiting for that dazzling picture to cross the old telephone network. A smart browser displays all the text in the incoming HTML file from the Web site before requesting corresponding graphic files from the Web site. This allows users to scroll through the text of the document as the graphic files are arriving at their computers.

Those graphic files, however, must be in a file format that is understood by the browser. Typically, most browsers know how to present graphic files that are in the GIF file format. This format is specially designed to reduce the size of the file while losing none of the information—a perfect combination for the fast-moving superhighway.

The idea of fetching files from a remote Web site, then letting the browser software on your computer do the work of displaying the file and interacting with you severely limits the services Web sites can offer. Based on our experience in the workplace, we expect to be able to have complete interactive capability with any Web site. That is, we expect to use a Web site as a remote database and to provide quick, interactive responses similar to those we receive in game software.

Business computer networks are moving toward a client/server network, where the client computer requests information from a server. The server runs the program to respond to the request then sends the client computer the results of this processing. All the complex software necessary to meet the client's expectations resides on the server.

In contrast, a Web site server is like a big, remote hard disk shared among millions of computers, and the only service the server provides is transferring a requested file. All the sophisticated software necessary to meet any of the client's requests must reside on that computer, not the Web site server. This major difference between a business computer network and the Internet is keeping the full potential of the World Wide Web from being realized.

Software developers such as Microsoft and Sun Microsystems Inc. realize this limitation and have begun a concerted effort to remedy the problem by embellishing the capabilities of browser software. Their solution is to distribute various kinds of engines with the browser. An *engine,* sometimes called a *player,* is the software that can interpret the special code embedded in the HTML file that the browser doesn't understand. The browser then calls on these engines to perform animation, play sound, and interact with a database.

While software houses, such as Sun Microsystems Inc., are ensuring that the engines are included in browsers, they are also creating new computer languages that Web site developers can use to take advantage of these engines. One of the first of these languages, Java, was created by Sunsoft, the software division of Sun Microsystems Inc.

Java comes in two forms: Java and JavaScript. Both follow most of the C and C++ language conventions. Java is a compiled language and JavaScript is an interpretive language. Web site developers can use a variety of languages to create their Web pages. However, the computer understands only one language, called machine language. *Machine language* has all those ones and zeros that we've all heard about.

Two special programs convert Web site development languages into machine language—the compiler and the interpreter. The difference is that a *compiler* does its work before the visitor calls the Web page, while the *interpreter* performs the conversion while the visitor reads the Web page.

Applications developed in either form can be used by the latest version of the Netscape browser and Microsoft's Internet Explorer browser.

The other new language is VB Script, which was created by Microsoft using some of the Visual Basic language conventions. VB Script is an interpretive language that can be used with Microsoft's Internet Explorer, which is available at no cost by downloading the files from Microsoft's own Web site: www.microsoft.com/vbscript/.

Both languages expand the capabilities of the browser by offering Web site developers like you those features found in most computer languages: program flow control, information storage, and interaction with the software user.

LOOK AT THE WEB SITE KIT BILL GATES HAS FOR YOU

Microsoft is offering those looking to enter cyberspace a wealth of tools to help reach their destination. These range from the Internet Explorer, which is a smart browser that carries you through the Internet, to the Internet Assistant and other tools that help you create your own Web site. Then there is the sprinkle of Internet magic provided by VB Script.

VB Script expands the capability of Web sites built with HTML to include versatility truly worth any cyberspacenaut's visit to your Web site. VB Script is a close relative of Visual Basic for Applications, which is distributed with Microsoft Office. Therefore, anyone familiar with Visual Basic for Applications, or Visual Basic itself, will feel right at home with VB Script.

A complete tutorial of the VB Script language is presented throughout chapters of this book. So you can brush up on your Visual Basic skills or simply plunge right into learning VB Script from scratch, then go out and build a classy Web site.

Those of you who have dabbled with Java are not left out of Microsoft's Internet plan. VB Script can also use Java objects called applets. A Java *applet* is a compiled Java application.

The developers at Microsoft have given serious consideration to making VB Script separate from the browser. Microsoft has arranged with browser manufacturers to distribute the VB Script engine as helper software to the browser. The VB Script engine is actually a stand-alone executable file that is called by the browser whenever special code within the HTML file requires execution of the VB Script. At that point the browser executes the VB Script engine, which in turn compiles and runs the VB Script, then returns control back to the HTML file.

Upgrades to the VB Script engine can be installed easily without having to upgrade or change browsers. Likewise, you can change the browser without worrying about the VB Script engine. They are separate but compatible.

A Little Reality about Your Web Site and Web Browsers

Bill Gates's VB Script is a magic wand for your Web site but it will not perform miracles. There are technology limitations that even Bill Gates cannot easily overcome. The first obstacle is the browser. Each visitor to your Web site has a browser. Some of these browsers have the VB Script engine, others don't. Those without the VB Script engine will not be able to utilize the bit of magic you created in VB Script.

Enhancements made to the VB Script engine can easily be incorporated in the scripts on your Web site, but this too may be for naught. The VB Script engine residing on each user's computer must be upgraded to be able to properly use the enhancements. Simply, if the millions of Internet users don't keep their VB Script engines up to date, then they and you won't be able to fully take advantage of enhancements forthcoming to the VB Script language.

Don't rush out to incorporate Java into your Web site, thinking that the compatibility and upgradability problems with browsers will go away. Java has the same problem as VB Script.

Another taste of reality comes with the script that produces the magic for you. No magician would allow nosy members of the audience to sneak behind the scenes to learn how the tricks are performed. The same holds true with the magic that you create on your Web site. However, unlike a magician, you cannot keep out those unwanted peering eyes.

HTML files are specially coded text files that can be viewed with any text editor. VB Scripts are embedded directly into the HTML file and therefore can be read with any text editor. When the browser connects to your Web site, the HTML file is copied to the other computer and can be saved to a disk by the user. The file can then be picked apart by using a text editor, so everyone can see how you perform your Web site tricks.

Don't become overly concerned. Although your techniques for exploiting VB Script can be out in the open, no one except you can modify the files on your Web site. That is, the user can explore the copy of your file and make modifications. However, the modified file cannot be returned to your Web site.

VB Script adds a powerful capability to your HTML files on your Web site, but the language lacks some of the more advanced features that programmers have come to expect from a computer language. For example, VB Script is not object-oriented and does not offer interesting features such as inheritance, polymorphism, and operator overloading, which are the mainstays of such languages as C++.

Don't let any of these limitations prevent you from plunging into the new world of VB Script. As you'll see throughout these chapters, the shortcomings presented here are overshadowed by the new magic the VB Script places in your hands.

VB SCRIPT SPEAKS YOUR LANGUAGE

By now you are a little more than curious about VB Script. Enough of the hype, let's glimpse VB Script before embarking on learning this powerful addition to your Web authoring toolbox. Example 1.1 contains a brief sample of a VB Script embedded in a standard HTML file. This is a very basic game that can easily be expanded by using graphics, but you can do that after reading this book.

Example 1.1 A Simple HTML File with an Embedded VB Script

```
<HTML>
<HEAD><TITLE>What's Behind The Doors</TITLE>
<SCRIPT LANGUAGE="VBS">
<
Sub Submit_OnClick
    Dim Game
    Set Game = Document.GameBoard
    If IsNumeric(Game.Text1.Value) Then
        If Game.Text1.Value < 1 Or Game.Text1.Value > 3 Then
            MsgBox " Pick Door 1, 2 or 3."
        Else
            If Game.Text1.Value = 1 Then
                MsgBox "You win a trip to Europe!"
            Else
                If Game.Text1.Value = 2 Then
                    MsgBox "You win a trip to the mall!"
                Else
                    MsgBox "You win a trip home!"
```

```
                End If
            End If
      End If
    Else
        MsgBox "Please enter a numeric value."
    End If
End Sub
>
</SCRIPT>
</HEAD>
<BODY>
<FORM NAME="GameBoard">
Pick Door 1, 2 or 3.:
<INPUT NAME="Text1" TYPE="TEXT" SIZE="1">
<INPUT NAME="Submit" TYPE="BUTTON" VALUE="Submit">
</FORM>
</BODY>
</HTML>
```

The HTML file begins with a few HTML tags, the first of which, <HTML>, identifies the file to the browser as an HTML file. This tag is followed by two tags, <HEAD> and <TITLE>, which signify that the following text is to be treated as the title of the application. Notice that the line ends with a </TITLE> tag, which tells the browser that it has reached the end of the title.

Now comes a little VB Script magic. The <SCRIPT LANGUAGE= "VBS"> tag begins the segment of the HTML file that contains the VB Script. Actually, this line signals the browser to call for help from the VB Script language engine. Remember, the browser cannot interpret the VB Script language.

The script itself contains the definition of a procedure called Submit_OnClick. The end of the script is marked by another HTML tag, </SCRIPT>. This procedure is not executed until the user clicks on the Submit button on the form. Instead, the procedure is stored in memory for later use. All procedures must be defined in the HTML file before the procedure is called by the browser. This is why the procedure precedes the HTML code in the file.

Once the script is defined, the program returns to the standard HTML code to display a form on the screen. The form collects two pieces of information from the user. First is the guess of the door number, followed by a click on the Submit button. The browser stores the one-digit guess to an HTML variable called Text1.

When the Submit button is clicked, the browser calls the VB Script procedure Submit_OnClick. Inside the procedure, the script recognizes the form called GameBoard then reads the value that is assigned to the Text1 HTML variable to determine if the value is a number. If so, the script determines if the number is within the acceptable range of doors. If so, the script compares the number to numbers on the door, and if a match occurs, an appropriate message is displayed in a message box on the screen. If any step fails, the script displays another message on the screen.

GETTING READY TO IMPROVE YOUR WEB PAGE

Don't be alarmed if you find Example 1.1 confusing. Unless you are an experienced programmer, the combination of HTML code and the VB Script language in the same application can easily make you close the cover of this book and head for the television. Stop! There's probably nothing on but reruns anyway. Stick around and we'll make any confusion you may have disappear in a matter of pages.

This chapter is just a warm-up for hot, new, and exciting things to come. By now some of the magic of cyberspace has disappeared. Before you become disillusioned, remember your job is to master the tricks of cyberspace and dazzle everyone who visits your Web site. Your job isn't to be dazzled yourself.

Whenever I set out to teach someone a new skill such as VB Script, a big question always must be answered. What can I assume the reader knows? If I assume the reader knows HTML coding—and he or she doesn't—then the reader is lost trying to learn VB Script. I don't want to lose any reader, so I've included one chapter that primes everyone on the HTML standard. Only one chapter? Believe me, HTML isn't that difficult to learn, and one chapter is more than enough preparation for VB Script.

We move quickly from HTML into the fundamentals of the VB Script language: variables, constants, expressions, statements, and operators. Then we enter into flow control, which is illustrated in Example 1.1. After that, the topics turn to more complex issues, such as arrays, strings, moving data in and out of the HTML page, and built-in functions. You'll find that VB Script is loaded with useful functions that take the pain out of programming complex applications.

Well, it seems time to begin the first lesson in VB Script. Sit back and let the magic carpet trip into cyberspace begin!

Chapter 2

HTML and Your Web Page

Golly Gee, Do I Have to Be a Programmer?

Before you can wave the VB Script magic wand on your Web site, you must master the hypertext markup language, better known as HTML. This is the only language that browsers understand and, therefore, the language used to create Web pages.

You may think programming a computer is beyond your capabilities. Learning all those bits and bytes is not what you had in mind when you thought of creating your own piece of cyberspace when you purchased this book. Put aside your fears. HTML is the simplest of all programming languages, which anyone can master within a few hours.

HTML has only two components, called *elements*: markup tags and character entities. These fancy words can be confusing but their meanings are familiar. A *markup tag* is a special code that represents a direction. Think of it as an abbreviation such as L for left turn and R for right turn. A *character entity* is text that appears on the screen.

The basic concept of HTML is to place markup tags into a standard word processing file, called a *text file*, to tell the browser how to display the text on the screen. Actually, HTML can tell the browser to display more than text, such as lines, push buttons, graphics, and other features that are found in most Web sites.

THE FIRST PIECE OF YOUR WEB PAGE KIT

If you are afraid of programming your Web site, authoring tools can take over the chore of inserting the markup tags into your Web page. You'll still have to give the tool instructions by changing the style of the text on the Web page or selecting the appropriate options from the menu.

There are generally two kinds of Web page authoring tools: a stand-alone software package, such as HoTMetaL Pro, and a template that enhances the capability of a word processing software package, such as Microsoft's Internet Assistant for Word for Windows.

A stand-alone authoring tool provides space to enter the text of your Web page, then lets you pick options from a menu bar to insert the fancy features of HTML. You can review your Web page while it is under construction by selecting another option from the menu bar. Some authoring tools are also Web browsers, so the tool switches hats and displays the contents of the page as a browser would display it on a visitor's computer.

Other authoring tools lack a built-in browser simulator. Instead, the authoring software calls your browser, such as Netscape, if a browser exists on your computer. However, keep in mind that the millions who will visit your Web site may have different browsers than the one available with your authoring tool, and, therefore, the appearance of your page could be different than what appears on your computer screen.

The authoring tools in the form of templates for word processing software, such as Microsoft Word for Windows, enable you to have the word processing software insert the markup tags into your text. First, open the document as an HTML document. You are given this choice when you select File, New from the menu bar. Next, enter the text of your page using your word processor.

Highlight each line of text and select the appropriate HTML style from the style drop-down Edit box that appears below the menu bar. The HTML markup code is placed on that line for you by the template. Other features, such as inserting graphics and calling other files from your page, are achieved by selecting the desired feature from the Insert menu item.

As with the stand-alone Web page authoring tool, you can see the page through the eyes of the browser by toggling a button on the menu bar. This changes the view of the document from development to browser and back to development. A word of caution: The techniques just described are those typically used by Web page authoring tools. However, the tool you select might use a different method of development than these. Make sure you read the documentation that came with your software to learn how to properly use the package to build your Web page.

Authoring tools, like browsers, allow you to use the features of HTML that were standardized at the time the authoring tool was produced. HTML is an evolving language; therefore, expect enhancements to this language—enhancements that won't be available to you unless you update your authoring tool.

However, you can get around this problem by inserting the appropriate markup tags into the document yourself. Yes, it is time to become an HTML programmer. It's really not that bad, as you'll see in this chapter.

You don't need a fancy Web page authoring tool to create a Web page. In fact, NotePad, an editor distributed free as part of Microsoft Windows, is a perfect tool to use to create a Web page. Any text editor will do and any word processor will also do as long as the file is saved as a text (.txt) file. A text file contains no word processing format command (commands hidden in the file that tell the word processing software how to display the text on the screen). The same concept—with different commands—is used in the HTML language.

How are markup tags placed into your Web page? Just type these special codes into the file on the appropriate lines. It is that simple—and we'll show you how to perform this magic throughout this chapter.

THE TRICKS OF A SIMPLE WEB PAGE

The magic of a Web page lies in the clever use of markup tags. Use them properly and your visitors will be dazzled. Use them poorly and they'll soon be hitting the cyberspace road to find a more attractive Web site. So what are these markup tags? How can you master this trick?

Before learning this specialty, you need a firm understanding of the concept of a markup tag and how these tags are used to define a Web page. A markup tag is a special symbol to define how text is to be displayed on the screen by the browser.

Each markup tag begins with a less than (<) symbol and ends with a greater than (>) symbol. Between these symbols are the code letters of the markup tag. Markup tags are normally entered into a Web page in pairs. The first markup tag is placed ahead of the text that is affected by the tag. The second markup tag is placed at the end of the affected text. This way the browser knows where to begin and end the display of the text. The pair of markup tags are nearly identical, except that the second markup tag contains a forward slash (/) as the first character before the code letters.

We said that a Web page is similar to a word processing file. The file contains text and control characters that direct how the word processor is going to display the text on the screen. These control characters are called *markup tags* in HTML.

A standard text file—a file without control characters—is transformed into a Web page by placing a specific pair of markup tags in the file. These markup tags are <HTML> and </HTML>. Example 2.1 contains a skeleton of a Web page that shows only these markup tags. Not much, you might say! And you are correct. However, these markup tags are all that is required to created a Web page for your Web site.

Example 2.1 The Skeleton of a Web Page File

```
<HTML>
</HTML>
```

Save these markup tags in a file called index.html, transfer the file to your Web site, and you will have created your first Web page. However,

The index.html File

What Kind of File Name Is index.html?

If you read the text carefully, you noticed that we instructed you to name your first Web page file index.html. Anyone familiar with a PC immediately realizes that there is a problem with that file name. There are four characters in the file extension. DOS permits only three letters, so how can you create a file with a four-character extension? You can't in DOS.

The conflict is with the operating system used in cyberspace. Web servers don't use DOS; instead, they use UNIX. The UNIX operating system permits four-character extensions. (Actually, there is no file extension in UNIX.)

This problem is further complicated by the World Wide Web standard that requires the browser to request from every Web site the file index.html. This is the only file that the browser knows exists on the Web site. The index.html file contains instructions for the browser to load other files related to the Web site as needed.

So here is the problem: Web pages created on a PC cannot save a file as index.html and browsers will look only for a file called index.html. The solution is to save the file on the PC as index.htm. Transfer the file to the Web site, then copy the file to index.html (cp index.htm index.html).

Making index.html Accessible

Just transferring your Web page file to your directory on the Web site server doesn't make your Web page available to visitors to the site. You still must perform a few pieces of magic to make your Web page visible.

First, the index.html file (and all your other Web page files) must be located in the public_html directory on the Web site server. If you transferred the files into a different directory, you can move the files into the public_html directory by using the UNIX command mv (mv index.html public_html).

Hold on! You must perform one final magic trick. Tell UNIX that the file must be accessible to all your friends—and strangers—who visit the Web site. You do this by using the UNIX command chmod (chmod 755 index.html). The numbers represent the permissions you are granting to your visitors, and index.html, of course, is the name of the file that will be accessed by visitors. Each file on your Web site must be made accessible by using this technique.

don't expect much! A visitor can visit your Web site but will see nothing on the screen—the file contains no text! We'll take care of this problem throughout this chapter.

PLEASE SAY SOMETHING!

You won't make anyone happy by offering an empty Web page. How about adding some text? You can do this by simply using another pair of markup tags: <BODY> and </BODY>. These markup tags are used to define the body of a Web page and are placed between the pair of <HTML> tags.

The text is then placed between the <BODY> markup tags. This is shown in Example 2.2, which enhances the previous example with a phrase every programmer knows, "Hello, world!" (For those who are not programmers, the first program learned in nearly every computer language displays the phrase "Hello, world!" on the screen.)

Example 2.2 Adding Text to the Web Page

```
<HTML>
<BODY>
Hello, world!
</BODY>
</HTML>
```

Any characters that appear within the <BODY> markup tag are actually displayed on the screen, untouched by the browser. Well, there are exceptions. The browser determines the size of the characters, the font, and the style of the characters. As author of the Web page, you don't get to make these choices at least in Example 2.2. Later in this chapter, you'll learn how to control the presentation of the text.

The other exception occurs when other markup tags are inserted into the body of the Web page. Those markup tags are not displayed but instead are interpreted by the browser as further instructions for the display of the Web page.

HOKUS POKUS, CHANGE THIS FONT

Just plain text on the screen does little to impress visitors, no matter how much the browser tries to use the default settings to make your information pleasant to read. Let's try to change drab text into something that will get a "wow" from visitors to your Web site.

An assorted group of markup tags can be used to specify the appearance of the text on your Web page. Let's begin by looking at markup tags that determine the font style used. Font style consists of regular, bold, italic, and underlined. Text placed within the body of the Web page is displayed in the regular font style by default. This means that you don't need to use any special markup tag to get this result.

The bold font style is specified by embedding the bold markup tag in the Web page. The symbols for the bold markup tags are <B> and </B>. Text placed between these markup tags will appear in bold on the screen.

Likewise, the italic markup tags, <I> and </I>, are used to have the browser display the text that appears between the italics. Underlined text is displayed in a similar manner, by using the <U> and </U> markup tags. Example 2.3 shows the markup tags to display the phrase "Hello, world!" in each of these font styles.

Example 2.3 Displaying Text in Various Font Styles

```
<HTML>
<BODY>
Hello, world!
<B> Hello, world! </B>
<I> Hello, world! </I>
<U> Hello, world! </U>
</BODY>
</HTML>
```

Specifying the font style for various pieces of text used on a Web page can become tedious for some Web page developers. This is especially true if you lack the talent for creative page design. Don't fret, HTML has a series of markup tags that are perfect for you. This series requires only that you determine the relative importance of each segment of the text. HTML then passes this information to the browser and lets the browser determine the font style and other characteristics of the text.

The first set of markup tags in this series is the header tags. These markup tags allow you to rank the importance of text from 1 through 6, with 1 being the most important text. Another way to look at this is as level of headings in a newspaper, magazine, or book.

The header tags are <H1> and </H1>. Notice that the ranking number appears as the last character in the markup tag. Subsequent header tags are <H2> and </H2>, <H3> and </H3>, and so on through <H6> and </H6>. Text that appears between these header tags is displayed appropriately by the browser.

Even though not a headline, special text also can be made to stand out on the page by using another set of markup tags. These are the emphasis tag, the strong tag, and the citation tag.

The emphasis tag is symbolized as <EM> and </EM>, the strong tag uses <STRONG> and </STRONG>. Both markup tags ask the browser to use the browser's default text characteristics to bring out the text appearing between the tags. The emphasis-tagged text is outstanding among the rest of the text, and the strong-tagged text really pops out at the visitor.

In contrast, the citation tag, symbolized as <CITE> and </CITE>, emphasizes text as either italics or underlined by most browsers. The choice is left to the browser and not the Web page author. Example 2.4 illustrates the use of these markup tags.

You Don't Have to Shoot Blindly

Although you won't know exactly how your words are shown to the user, you can have some idea by using your authoring tool or your own browser. Browsers typically are set up to connect to your favorite Web site on startup. However, the browser can also be used while your computer is disconnected from cyberspace.

You can test your Web page by starting your browser, then opening the Web page file using the File, Open menu options in the browser. The browser will then search your local hard disk for the file instead of heading out into cyberspace. If you don't like what you see, you can always close down the browser and redesign your Web page.

Example 2.4 Emphasizing Text on the Web Page

```
<HTML>
<BODY>
<H1> Hello, world! </H1>
<H2> Hello, world! </H2>
<H3> Hello, world! </H3>
<H4> Hello, world! </H4>
<H5> Hello, world! </H5>
<H6> Hello, world! </H6>
<EM> Hello, world! </EM>
<STRONG> Hello, world! </STRONG>
<CITE> Hello, world! </CITE>
</BODY>
</HTML>
```

All this fancy text may not be what you want for your Web page. Strange as this may seem, sometimes simple, plain text makes the text different enough to get the attention of the visitor and it is easier to read. If this is what you want, two markup tags are right for you. These are the code tag and the typewriter tag. Both direct the browser to use a monospaced font to display the text.

In a monospaced font each character of text receives the same space on the screen. Many fonts used by graphical user interfaces (GUIs) such as Microsoft Windows use proportionally spaced fonts. Here, the space reserved for a character is proportional to the width of the character. This means the letter *i* will have half the space of the letter *a*, and the letter *w* will have nearly double the space as the letter *a*.

The code tag is symbolized with <CODE> and </CODE>. The name of this tag comes from the term *computer program code*, which is a style of text used to display a program listing. The typewriter tag uses the <TT> and </TT> symbols and is named after the font used in a typewriter.

You can add special treatment to your Web page text by using another set of markup tags: the strikeout tag, the block quotes tag, and two tags found on a Netscape-capable browser—the font tag and the blink tag.

Let's begin with the strikeout tag. This markup tag, <STRIKE> and </STRIKE>, is used to display text with a line through the text. This can be used to indicate that the text has been marked for deletion, as in a document. The block quotes markup tag uses <BLOCKQUOTE> and </BLOCKQUOTE> to place quotations around text that appears between these markup tags. The authors of Netscape built the blink tag and the font tag into their browser. A word of caution: Not all browsers will recognize these markup tags, although many newer browsers are Netscape capable.

The font tag (<FONT SIZE=12> and </FONT>) is used to specify the size of the font in which the Web page author wants to display the text that appears between these markup tags. Notice that the font tag has an attribute called SIZE. An attribute is not a markup tag. Instead, an *attribute* is assigned a keyword or value that defines a characteristic of the markup tag. In this case, the attribute is used to set the size of the font as 12-point type. As is obvious from the name, the blink tag (<BLINK> and </BLINK>) directs the browser to flash the text that appears between the markup tags on the screen.

Not all the text that appears on the Web page is contained in the body of the page. That is, many Web pages have a page heading and title that appear above the body of the text of the page. Page heads and titles are created by using the <HEAD> and </HEAD> and <TITLE> and </TITLE> markup tags. A word of caution: These markup tags must appear above the <BODY> markup tag on the Web page. Example 2.5 shows the proper format for using monospaced tags, strikeout tags, block quote tags, the font tags, the blink tags, and the head and title tags.

Example 2.5 Additional Ways to Improve the Display of Text on the Web Page

```
<HTML>
<HEAD><TITLE>My First HTML Program</TITLE></HEAD>
<BODY>
<CODE> Hello, world! </CODE>
<TT> Hello, world! </TT>
<STRIKE> Hello, world! </STRIKE>
<BLOCKQUOTE> Hello, world! </BLOCKQUOTE>
<FONT SIZE=12>Hello, world! </FONT>
<BLINK> Hello, world! </BLINK>
</BODY>
</HTML>
```

GRAB YOUR MAGIC PAINT BRUSH

The illusion of a classy Web page has a lot to do with how you employ color on your Web site. So far in our exploration of HTML, we were able to dress up our Web page of text by specifying font styles and other characteristics. This is a big improvement over our previous Web page, but something is still missing. We need something that will give the Web page pizzazz!

You can perform two tricks that will deliver this pizzazz to your visitors. These are color and an image that will be used as the background for the page. A word of caution before we proceed: HTML does not have standard markup tags that direct the browser to perform these tricks. Instead, the authors of Netscape created attributes to the <BODY> markup tag to give you this control of your Web page. This means that these attributes are available only in Netscape-compatible browsers.

Some text on a Web page serves a dual purpose. First, the text communicates with the reader; second, it is used to link to other pieces of information that are contained in the same file, in another file on the same Web site, or in a file on a different Web site. This text is called *hypertext* and the connection to the other information is called a hypertext *link*. We now describe these more fully.

Three states can exist with hypertext: The text has not been selected, the text was already selected, or the text is the currently active link. Each state is identified to visitors by a unique color. You can specify these colors by using the appropriate attribute: LINK, VLINK, or ALINK. LINK is the color for hypertext links that have not been selected by the visitor; VLINK specifies the color of previously selected hypertext; ALINK is the color of the currently active hypertext link.

If you don't select a color or the browser does not recognize these color attributes, the browser will determine the colors of your page. Actually, the user can change the color preferences for these features of the browser. In such a case, your color selection overrides their choice only for your Web page.

Actually, only three colors can be used: red, green, and blue. The degree to which each color is displayed creates the palette of colors that we have come to expect from a Web site. The blend of red, green, and blue is specified as a value for each color that ranges between 0 and 255. If each of these colors is set at 0, then the text is displayed in the color black. In contrast, if the value is 255 for each color, then the text appears white.

Don't you wish life were so simple? It isn't. The color values assigned to the appropriate attribute of the <BODY> markup tag must be represented in a hexadecimal value. What? We won't get into this. Let's just say that the values 0 through 225 are decimal values and must be converted to a different kind of number. You can use the calculator that comes with Microsoft Windows to do the conversion for you. Table 2.1 provides a few of these settings.

Example 2.6 illustrates how these values are assigned to attributes of the <BODY> markup tag. Standard text is displayed in black, while those words that cause a jump to another piece of text are displayed in blue. Once a jump has occurred, the text color changes to green—unless it is the current link, in which case the text appears red. Also notice that the <BGCOLOR> markup tag is used to set the background color of the page to white.

Example 2.6 Assigning Colors to Text

```
<HTML>
<BODY BGCOLOR="#FFFFFF" TEXT="#000000" LINK="#0000FF" VLINK="#00FF00"
ALINK="#FF0000">
Hello, world!
</BODY>
</HTML>
```

Table 2.1 Sample Hexadecimal Color Values

Color	*Value*
White	FFFFFF
Cyan	00FFFF
Magenta	FF00FF
Yellow	FFFF00
Blue	0000FF
Green	00FF00
Red	FF0000
Dark gray	808080
Medium gray	A0A0A4
Cream	FFFBF0
Medium green	C0D0C0
Light blue	A6CAF0
Light gray	C0C0C0
Dark cyan	008080
Dark magenta	800080
Dark blue	000080
Dark yellow	808000
Dark green	008000
Dark red	800000
Black	000000

Converting from Decimal Values to Hexadecimal with the Microsoft Windows Calculator

1. Select the Calculator icon from the Accessories group.
2. Select the View menu option and change from standard view to scientific view.
3. Select the Dec radio button.
4. Enter the decimal value of the color setting, such as 255.
5. Select the Hex radio button to display the hexadecimal equivalent. Note that the calculator displays some hexadecimal values as letters.
6. Assign the hexadecimal value to the color setting of the attribute. Remember, three values are required. We only showed one value here.

There must be a better way to colorize the Web page, you may be thinking. The easiest method is to use a Web page authoring tool that enables you to change colors on the fly. Then, when you save the Web page, the authoring tool will handle all the value conversions for you.

Another important feature of the Netscape extensions is the ability to use a graphic image as the background for your page. This is made possible by using the BACKGROUND attribute of the <BODY> markup tag. The value assigned to the BACKGROUND attribute is the location and the name of the graphic file. We'll go into more detail about how to point to a graphic file, such as a picture, in the next section.

I Need Pictures!

So far we have only text with a little dabble of text emphasis and color. Where are the real tricks used on Web sites across cyberspace? Where are the pictures? Hold on, we're going to introduce you to the magic trick that can place your face—or any graphic—on your Web site for the whole world to see.

A graphic image is a digitized version of an image, like the familiar graphic images used as icons and the graphics that we can draw using various popular drawing packages such as Microsoft Paint and Corel Draw. These tools allow us to produce artwork directly on the computer and save the artwork to a file.

However, artwork can be developed on paper or in the form of a photograph, both of which can be digitized and stored as a file on the Web site server. This transformation is performed by hardware called a scanner. You can purchase a *scanner* or go to a service company that will scan your artwork or photos into a file so you can incorporate them on your Web page.

A serious drawback to using graphics on your Web page is that graphic files can be very large in terms of the number of bytes required to represent the image in the file. Remember, each byte used on your Web page must make the long journey through cyberspace from your Web site to your visitor's computer. It is easy to say that the larger the graphic file is, the longer it will take for your visitor to see the graphic. The question you must ask yourself is, Will the visitor have the patience to wait until the complete graphic file is received before moving on to the next Web site?

The key to improving the speed at which graphic files flow across the electronic superhighway is the file format used to store the graphic. You are probably used to seeing the extension BMP to represent a graphic file. This is the graphic file format used by Microsoft Windows. However, an improved graphic file format called GIF is used for graphic files on the Internet. So, it is your job to make sure that all graphic files you use in your Web page are in the GIF format. If they are not, use a graphical software package to convert the graphic file to the GIF format.

A graphic file is included in a Web page by using the <IMG> markup tag. This is illustrated in Example 2.7, where the browser is instructed to return to the Web site for the graphic file mast.gif. This file is then loaded into the computer and displayed on the screen. Notice that the name of the file is assigned the attribute SRC, indicating the source of the graphic file.

What if the graphic file isn't found on the Web site server? Although this will rarely occur if you are a good, thoughtful Web site owner, you can use another attribute, ALT, to have the browser display text in place of the graphic file. This too is shown in Example 2.7.

Example 2.7 Inserting a Graphic File into Your Web Page

```
<HTML>
<BODY>
<IMG SRC="mast.gif" ALT="File is not available at this time.">
</BODY>
</HTML>
```

Inserting an image into a Web page requires a little more than simply using the <IMG> markup tag and the SRC attribute. The results may be a little disappointing, since the browser drops the image on the page with little regard for the surrounding text. Believe me, this can leave an unsightly Web page, one that will show you are an amateur cyberspace magician.

You can avoid this pitfall by using the ALIGN attribute. The ALIGN attribute is assigned a value that instructs the browser how to align the graphic with the text. Three standard values can be used with the ALIGN attribute: "top", "middle", and "bottom" (The quotation marks must be included when using values.) The "top" value causes the image to be aligned with the top of the tallest element in the text line that surrounds the image. The "middle" value has the browser center the image between the top and the baseline of the surrounding text or center the text on the image, if it's larger. And "bottom" aligns the image with the baseline at the text.

As you can imagine, when the Netscape folks got ahold of the ALIGN attribute, they discovered these values to be very limiting. Fortunately, they added a little magic potion of their own, which you can use with your Web page, assuming that most browsers will conform to the Netscape standards. Table 2.2 contains these values.

In addition to providing improved values for the ALIGN attribute, Netscape added a few of its own attributes: BORDER, HSPACE, VSPACE, WIDTH, and HEIGHT. The BORDER attribute is assigned an integer value that defines the thickness of the border surrounding the image. A value of zero removes the border from the screen.

The HSPACE and VSPACE attributes are used to define the amount of (horizontal or vertical) space that the browser should leave between the image and the page margin or the text. These attributes are assigned integer values. The HSPACE attribute sets the spacing between the alignment margin and the image and between the adjoining text and the image. The VSPACE attributes sets the space between the text and the top and bottom of the image.

Table 2.2 Netscape Extensions for the ALIGN Attribute

Value	*Description*
"left"	Places the image on the left margin of the page and wraps the text around the right side of the image
"right"	Places the image on the right margin of the page and wraps the text around the left side of the image
"texttop"	Aligns the image with the tallest text in the line that surrounds the image, which is not always the same as the standard value "top"
"absmiddle"	Aligns the image with the center of the text that surrounds the image
"absbottom"	Aligns the image with the bottom of the text that surrounds the image

One of the important extensions to HTML added by Netscape is the ability to define the width and height of the image on the screen. Integer values are used for the WIDTH and HEIGHT attributes. If these attributes are not included in the Web page, the browser will not adjust the size of the graphic for display purposes. Example 2.8 contains some of the Netscape extensions to the HTML standard.

Example 2.8 Fine Tuning the Graphic Image on the Screen

```
<HTML>
<BODY>

<IMG SRC="mast.gif" ALT="File is not available at this time"
ALIGN="right" WIDTH=5 HEIGHT=8>

</BODY>
</HTML>
```

CAN WE DRESS UP THE WEB PAGE A LITTLE MORE?

You can weave still more magic on your Web page. Let's turn our attention to the layout of the text on the page. You can improve the appearance of the page by arranging the text in clever ways. For example, you can have text centered by the browser by using the <CENTER> and </CENTER> markup tags. Text placed between these markup tags is automatically centered on the line.

Sometimes a block of text is not the ideal layout for a section of your page. A list of data is more appropriate. HTML offers several ways to format your text into a list through an assortment of markup tags. Let's begin our review of this ingredient of your magic potion with the directory list tag. This markup tag is symbolized with <DIR> and </DIR>, and requires the related markup tag <LI>, which is used to identify each item on the list.

The <DIR> markup tag tells the browser that the following text must be displayed in a list format on the screen. The <LI> markup tag precedes the name of each item. Example 2.9 shows how these markup tags are used in the HTML Web page.

Example 2.9 Creating a Directory List

```
<HTML>
<BODY>
<DIR><LI>Bob<LI>Mary<LI>Mary</DIR>
</BODY>
</HTML>
```

Another type of list available with HTML is a definition list, which consists of two columns. The first column contains a word or expression that is explained by the text in the second column. Three sets of markup tags are used to create a definition list. These are <DL> and </DL>, <DT> and </DT>, and <DD> and </DD>.

The <DL> markup tag alerts the browser that the following text must be displayed as a definition list. The <DT> markup tag precedes each word or expression that is to be defined. The <DD> markup tag precedes the text that provides the definition. Example 2.10 illustrates this technique.

Example 2.10 Creating a Definition Listing

```
<HTML>
<BODY>

<DL><DT>Car</DT><DD> A car is a type of vehicle.</DD><DT>Sentra</DT><DD>
A Sentra is a type of car.</DT></DL>

</BODY>
</HTML>
```

The previous two examples consisted of unordered lists. An *unordered* list is one where there is no significance to the placement of the item on the list. In contrast, an *ordered list* is where items are identified by letters of the alphabet or a sequence of numbers. HTML can be used to have the browser order the list for you by using the <OL> and <LI> markup tags.

The <OL> markup tag sets the stage for the browser to order the text that follows; the <LI> markup tag is used in the same way as it is used in the previous list, that is, to identify the text of each item on the list.

Our friends at Netscape have taken this concept a step further and created an attribute for the <OL> markup tag called TYPE. This attribute is assigned a keyword that symbolizes the letters or numbers that are to be used for the list. Table 2.3 contains a list of these keywords. Netscape also provides the START attribute, which accepts a specific index that is used by the browser when displaying the list. For example, assigning the value of 10 to the START attribute causes the browser to begin the list with the number 10 assigned to the first item on the list. Example 2.11 shows the proper way to use the ordered list markup tag in a Web page.

Example 2.11 Creating an Ordered List

```
<HTML>
<BODY>
<OL TYPE="1" START="10"><LI>Bob<LI>Mary<LI>Mary</OL>
</BODY>
</HTML>
```

It is common to display an unorganized list of items with a graphic character beginning the line of each new item, especially when these lines contain more than a few words. This is sometimes called a *bulleted list*. You can easily transform your list of items into a bulleted list. Actually, you have a choice between a solid bullet, called a "disc"; an open bullet, called

Table 2.3 Keywords for the TYPE Attribute of the Ordered List Markup Tag

Keyword	*Description*
"a"	Use lowercase letters for list
"A"	Use uppercase letters for list
"i"	Use small roman numerals for list
"I"	Use capital roman numerals for list
"1"	Use arabic numerals for list (this is the default)

a "circle"; or a square bullet, called a "square". This is all made possible by using the unordered list tag along with the Netscape-added attribute TYPE. As you can imagine, the value assigned to TYPE is the keyword: "disc", "circle", or "square".

The symbols used to describe the unordered list are very similar to that of the ordered list, except that the <OL> markup tag is replaced by <UL> and the values assigned to the TYPE attribute are appropriate to the unordered list. Example 2.12 shows how this is done.

Example 2.12 Creating an Unordered Bulleted List

```
<HTML>
<BODY>

<UL TYPE="disc"><LI>Bob<LI>Mary<LI>Mary</UL>

</BODY>
</HTML>
```

Still another type of list that can be incorporated into your Web page is a menu. This is created nearly identically to the directory list shown in Example 2.9, except that the markup tags <DIR> and </DIR> are replaced with <MENU> and </MENU>.

In addition to breaking up blocks of text by using ordered and unordered lists, other techniques can be used to achieve similar results. For example, you can divide the text into paragraphs by using the <P> and </P> markup tags to identify the beginning and end of the paragraph.

Another dramatic method is to place a horizontal rule between key components of the Web page text. This is accomplished by using the horizontal rule tag <HR> wherever you desire a rule to be placed across the page.

The horizontal rule tag has several attributes that can be modified. These are ALIGN, SIZE, WIDTH, and NOSHADE. The ALIGN attribute can be assigned the keyword "left", "right", or "center", which positions the rule on the page. The SIZE attribute is assigned a value equal to the number of pixels that make up the thickness of the line, and the WIDTH attribute is assigned the number of pixels that make up the length of the line. The NOSHADE attribute is not assigned a keyword or value. Simply the presence of this attribute causes the browser to display a solid rule rather than the standard shaded engraved rule, which is the default setting.

Throughout this section we explored ways to break up blocks of text that appear on a Web page. However, sometimes the browser will do this for you—and you won't be appreciative. This occurs when the browser begins a new page in an inappropriate place. You can't stop the browser from doing this; however, you can limit this destruction by providing the browser with a little direction.

Review your page very carefully to determine where the browser is likely to insert page breaks. You may even consider displaying the page in your browser to find these natural page breaks. When you come across an inappropriate page break, insert a page break of your own with the page break markup tag <BR>.

For those browsers that conform to the Netscape standard, you can direct the browser to keep text together by using the no-break tag. Text that appears between <NOBR> and </NOBR> will be moved to the next page if there is no room to fit the entire block of text on the page.

FORGET ABOUT THE CHAIRS! I WANT TABLES ON MY WEB PAGE

After learning how to perform the magic to transform block text on your Web page into a list of items, you probably already know that there must be another trick to create a full-fledged table on the page. You're right, and now is the time for us to share this trick with you.

A table consists of rows and columns that form individual cells on the screen. This is similar to a spreadsheet in appearance and available only with Netscape-compatible browsers. A word of caution: Some Web page authoring tools don't support this feature, leaving you to enter a table into your Web site by hand.

Now for some magic. The browser is alerted to display a table by the table markup tags <TABLE> and </TABLE>. Within these tags are placed other markup tags that actually give the table its structure. Two of the most important of these tag sets are <TR> and </TR> and <TD> and </TD>. These markup tags define the rows and the data cells. Columns are automatically created by the browser after reading these markup tags.

Another important set of markup tags is <TH> and </TH>. Typically these markup tags are used with the <TR> markup tag to specify column heads, although the markup tag can be used throughout the table.

Example 2.13 shows how to weave a simple table on your Web page. This table consists of three rows and two columns. The first row contains column heads of First Name and Last Name. The next two rows contain data for those columns. The browser is very forgiving. If you don't have sufficient data to fill a cell, the browser will place spaces in the cells for you.

Each table that you create should have a caption. Be sure to use the set of <CAPTION> and </CAPTION> markup tags to position a caption on your table. The text of the caption is entered between these markup tags.

Example 2.13 Creating a Table on Your Web Page

```
<HTML>
<TABLE>

<CAPTION>My Friends</CAPTION>

<TR><TH>First Name</TH><TH>Last Name</TH></TR>

<TR><TD>Mary</TD><TD>Jones</TD></TR>

<TR><TD>Tom</TD><TD>Smith</TD></TR>

</TABLE>
</HTML>
```

Now that you know how to build a simple table, let's explore the tricks that will make the table pop out at your visitor. The first trick is to place a border around the cells of the table. This is made possible by the BORDER attribute. The BORDER attribute can be assigned an integer that is proportional to the thickness of the border. A value of 5 tells the browser to make the border half as thick as a value of 10. You can experiment with these settings and see the results with your own browser. Or you can insert the attribute BORDER into the Web page and let the browser determine its thickness.

You can also specify the number of rows and columns that will be in the table without having to define the contents of the cells. This is made possible by using the ROWSPAN and the COLSPAN attributes and assigning the appropriate numbers to these attributes. The default value is one row and one column.

You can adjust the alignment of the various aspects of the table by assigning a value to the appropriate attribute. Cells can be modified by using the CELLPADDING and CELLSPACING attributes. CELLPADDING determines the space between the borders of the cell and the text in the cell. The default value is 1 and the padding can be increased proportionally by increasing this value. In contrast, CELLSPACING determines the spacing between cells in the table. The default value for this attribute is 2.

You can direct the browser to position text the way that you, not the browser, would like. Two key attributes give you this magical power: ALIGN and VALIGN. The ALIGN attribute can be assigned the keywords "left", "right", or "center," which positions the text horizontally within the cell. The VALIGN attribute can be assigned the keywords "top", "middle", "bottom", or "baseline" to have the browser move the text vertically in the cell.

A word of caution: If the text you place into a cell is too wide, the browser will automatically break the word and wrap around to the next line within the cell. You can prevent this from happening by using the NOWRAP attribute. Simply place this attribute within the <TABLE> markup tag and the browser will understand your desire. Example 2.14 shows how to incorporate some of these features into the table definition.

Example 2.14 Enhancing the Appearance of a Table on Your Web Page

```
<HTML>
<TABLE BORDER NOWRAP ROWSPAN="3" COLSPAN="2">

<CAPTION>My Friends</CAPTION>

<TR><TH>ALIGN="center" First Name</TH><TH> ALIGN="center" Last
Name</TH></TR>

<TR><TD> ALIGN="left" Mary</TD><TD> ALIGN="left" Jones</TD></TR>

<TR><TD> ALIGN="left" Tom</TD><TD> ALIGN="left" Smith</TD></TR>

</TABLE>
</HTML>
```

TIME TO GET A LITTLE HYPER

HTML is also used to tell the browser to quickly move to another part of the Web. This is called a *jump*. Remember, browsers retrieve files only from a Web site. When a request is made to visit a Web site, the browser is given the alias for the site such as www.microsoft.com. Once connected to the Web site, the browser will copy the index.html file from the Web site to the user's computer, then display the contents of the file on the screen.

Some of the text stands out from the rest by being displayed in a different color. This text is referenced to another part of the Web, such as a different part of the currently displayed HTML file or a different HTML file that still resides on the Web site. When a visitor points the cursor to the highlighted word then clicks the left mouse button, the browser will jump to the part of the Web that is specified by the highlighted text.

This concept is a key component of HTML and every Web site. You are probably familiar with hypertext from using the help facility of any Microsoft Windows application. Simply point and click, then magically the information you want will appear on the screen.

Example 2.15 exposes the trick of hypertext. The entire line is a markup tag called an anchor tag. An anchor tag defines the origin or destination of a hypertext link. Simply said, it gives the browser all the information necessary to create hypertext.

Example 2.15 A Hypertext Jump to Another File on the Same Web Site

```
<A HREF="bcn1.html">Bergen County Beat</A>
```

The beginning of an anchor tag is identified by the letter "A" and the end of the anchor tag is referenced by a "/A." Within these symbols are the two elements of the anchor tag, which are the name of the file and the text of the hypertext.

The HREF is an attribute of the anchor tag, assigned the name of the HTML file that will be copied from the Web site when the hypertext is selected by the user. In this example, the name of the file is bcn1.html. Notice that this name is contained within quotation marks. No path is given with this file name since the file is contained on the same Web site and in the same directory on the Web site server.

However, a jump can be made to anywhere on the World Wide Web, including a different Web site, by referencing the name of the Web site. This is illustrated in Example 2.16, where the hyperlink jumps to the Microsoft Web site that contains information about VB Script.

Example 2.16 A Hypertext Jump to Another Web Site

```
<A HREF="http://www.microsoft.com/vbscript/">VB Script</A>
```

In both examples, the text highlighted on the screen is contained within the greater than (>) and less than (<) symbols. In the first example, *Bergen County Beat* is the actual hypertext, while in the second example the hypertext is *VB Script*.

And, of course, the jump can be made to a place within the same file. This technique is shown in Example 2.17, where the jump is made to the section of the file identified as Pasta. As you can imagine, these are lines from a Web site file that displays the menu for a restaurant.

Example 2.17 A Hypertext Jump to a Portion of the Same File

```
<A HREF="#Pasta">Pasta</A>
.....
<A NAME="Pasta">Pasta</A>
```

The first line identifies the place to which to jump by using the hash symbol (#) in front of the name of the destination tag. Of course, this line also displays the hypertext *Pasta* on the screen. The next line actually appears somewhere else in the file. We just placed the line beneath the jump line for illustrative purposes. This line could appear anywhere in the file, including above the jump line.

This too is an anchor tag but contains the attribute NAME followed by the name of the anchor tag. This line also displays text on the screen using the same technique as shown in the jump line. Although this text is the same as the name of the anchor tag, any text could have been used.

CLICK ON THE PICTURE FOR THE JUMP

Probably one of the most dramatic tricks performed by Web site authors is to allow the visitor to click on a portion of a picture displayed on the screen, then have the browser display another file or another image. Let's see how this is done.

First, you'll need an image file in the GIF file format, which was discussed earlier in this chapter. Next, you'll need to create *hot spots* on this file. A hot spot is a segment of an image that when clicked on by a visitor is associated with another HTML file or image file. There are two methods for creating a hot spot: Use a hot spot editor or manually create the hot spot. Although most Web page authors prefer using a tool such as Thomas Boutell's Mapedit, we'll show you how to perform this same magic without a hot spot tool.

The image is divided into hot spots by referencing the pixels that define the segment. These values are placed into an image map file that is used by the browser to properly have your Web page respond to a visitor's selection.

Two kinds of image map can be created: HTTPS and HTTPD. The one you use for your image map depends on the server used for your Web site service. Check with your Web site service provider to determine which format is appropriate for your Web page. We'll use both formats in this section.

Both image map file formats require the same information. The only difference between them is the arrangement of the information in the image map file. Hot spots are categorized as rectangles, polygons, or circles. A rectangle hot spot is identified by two coordinates: the top left corner and the lower right corner of the hot spot. These are the values you must provide in the image map file.

A polygon hot spot is defined by "connecting the dots." That is, you provide the coordinates of two pixels on the image and the browser draws an imaginary line between these points. On the HTTPS server you can use an unlimited number of pixels. However, the HTTPD server limits you to 100 pixels.

The circle hot spot on the HTTPS server requires the coordinate of the pixel that is in the center of the circle and the radius. The radius value is

What Is a Pixel?

Pixel is the technical name for a picture element, or the smallest piece of information that can be displayed on a computer screen. Images on the screen appear to be solid lines, but in reality these solid lines are composed of tiny dots called pixels. The pixels are so small that they seem to blend together to form a solid image.

Each pixel is identified by coordinates of rows and columns. The top left corner of the image is identified as 0,0. Subsequent pixels on the zeroth (first) row are numbered 0,1; 0,2 ; and so on. Don't plan to sit in front of your screen and count pixels. A faster method of locating the number of a pixel is to display the image using graphic software.

For example, Paintbrush, which is supplied with Microsoft Windows in the Accessories group, can be used to identify pixel locations on an image. Here's how to use it:

1. Select the Paintbrush icon in the Accessories group.
2. Select View from the menu bar, then select Cursor Position. This will display the cursor position at the top of the window.
3. Select Options from the menu bar, then Image Attributes. Click on the pels radio button, then select OK.
4. Load the image into Paintbrush. Notice that as you move the cursor around the image, the corresponding cursor position value is displayed on the screen.

actually half the coordinate (the second number) because the first half of the coordinate is defined by the first coordinate that defines the center pixel. In contrast, the HTTPD server requires the full coordinates of the radius.

Examples 2.18 and 2.19 are typical image map files for the HTTPS and HTTPD servers, respectively. You'll notice that the first line in each file contains the default location of the Web site server. Each hot spot also contains the location and name of the file that will be loaded by the browser. The image map file should be saved under the same name as the image plus the extension "map." Once you have created the image map file, include the <IMG SRC="mast.gif" ISMAP="mast.map"> statement in the Web page using the technique described previously in this chapter.

Example 2.18 The Image Map for the HTTPS Server

```
default http://wisc.iss.com/directory/
rect (50,100), (300,200) http://wisc.iss.com/picture2.gif
poly(40,100), (150,200), (212,300) http://wisc.iss.com/file1.html
circle (211,100) 85 http://wisc.iss.com/file2.html
```

Example 2.19 The Image Map for the HTTPD Server

```
default http://wisc.iss.com/directory/
rect http://wisc.iss.com/picture2.gif 50,100  300,200
poly http://wisc.iss.com/file1.html 40,100 150,200 212,300
circle http://wisc.iss.com/file2.html 211,100 260,170
```

DON'T ASK QUESTIONS— JUST FILL OUT THE FORM

While wandering around cyberspace, you've probably stumbled across a Web site or two that displayed a fancy form on the screen, then asked you to complete the form. The form then was sent to the Web site author. Ever wonder how this trick is performed? Now the secret is out.

The form is actually a set of <FORM> and </FORM> markup tags. If you throw in a few associated markup tags and some magical attributes, you'll end up with a dramatic way to collect information from visitors to your Web site. The process of creating a form begins with including the form markup tags in your Web page.

Next, decide how you are going to collect information from the visitor. This can be in the format of straight text, check boxes, or radio buttons.

Example 2.20 illustrates a simple form that asks the visitor for identification, then provides area where multiline comments can be entered. The visitor completes the form and selects the Submit button, then the browser automatically sends the information to the Web site author via e-mail.

Example 2.20 A Sample Form with Responses Sent to an e-Mail Address

```
<HTML>
<BODY>

<H1>Sound Off!</H1>

<P>
Tell us what you like or dislike about your town, the county, the state,
On-Line New Jersey, or anything else. We may not be able to solve the
problem but we'll make sure you share your concerns with our readers.
Fill out this form then click on the Submit Query button.
<FORM ACTION="mailto:jimkeogh@soho.ios.com" METHOD="post">
<P>

First Name:      <INPUT NAME="Text2" VALUE="" MAXLENGTH="30" >
<P>

Last Name:      <INPUT NAME="Text3" VALUE="" MAXLENGTH="30" >
<P>

Street:              <INPUT NAME="Text4" VALUE="" MAXLENGTH="60" >
<P>

City:                 <INPUT NAME="Text5" VALUE="" MAXLENGTH="60" >
<P>

State:                <INPUT NAME="Text9" VALUE="" MAXLENGTH="2" >
<P>

Zip:                  <INPUT NAME="Text7" VALUE="" MAXLENGTH="15" >
<P>

Email Address: <INPUT NAME="Text8" VALUE="" MAXLENGTH="30" >
<P>

Comments:
<P>

<TEXTAREA NAME = "Textc" ROWS = 12 COLUMNS = 20 <INPUT NAME="Textc"
VALUE="" MAXLENGTH="500" > </TEXTAREA>
<P>
```

```
<INPUT TYPE="submit">  <INPUT TYPE="RESET">

</FORM>

</BODY>
</HTML>
```

Let's take apart this routine and see how each component works. After displaying a heading and instructions for completing the form, the form markup tag is inserted into the page. The ACTION attribute is assigned the keyword "mailto:" followed by the e-mail address that will receive the information entered into the form. This is the action that will take place when the visitor submits the form. The METHOD attribute is assigned the keyword "post", which tells the browser how to perform the action—post it to e-mail.

The next few lines prompt the visitor to enter single-line information. First is the label that describes the information, such as "First Name:". Following this is the <INPUT> markup tag that instructs the browser to read information from the keyboard. The NAME attribute is used to define an alias for the information entered by the visitor. In the first line, the first name of the visitor is represented throughout the page as "Text2". This is similar to a variable name in other computer languages.

The <INPUT> markup tag also uses the VALUE attribute. The VALUE attribute is assigned the default value for the NAME alias. Notice that two double quotation marks are assigned to the VALUE attribute (no space between the quotation marks). This means that there is no default value. Last, the MAXLENGTH attribute is used and assigned the value "30" to tell the browser not to accept more than 30 characters from the keyboard.

This pattern continues until the visitor is asked to enter free-form text under the heading "Comments." Since more than one line of text will be entered by the visitor, the browser must reserve a section of the page for collecting the information. The area is reserved by using the <TEXTAREA> markup tag.

The ROWS and COLUMN attribute values actually define the text area as being 20 characters wide and 12 lines deep. More than 12 lines of text can be entered but only 12 lines will be displayed at a time. The remaining lines can be displayed by using the vertical scroll bar provided by the browser.

Embedded in the <TEXTAREA> markup tag is the <INPUT> markup tag. Its attributes define the alias as "Textc", having no default value and having a maximum of 500 characters that can be entered by the visitor.

The form ends with the display of two additional input markup tags. Here, the TYPE attribute is used to define the user input as the Submit button and the Reset button. Other keywords that are used with the TYPE attribute are "radio", "checkbox", "password", or "text", which is the default value if the TYPE attribute is excluded in the input markup tag.

WHAT'S NEXT?

Well, you've learned many of the tricks you can perform with HTML. Now it is time to move forward with the latest technology—VB Script. The magic that you learned to perform in this chapter becomes the foundation to learn more advanced skills. The remainder of this book is devoted to teaching you how to master VB Script.

These new tricks enable you to create powerful Web pages that exploit the interactive capabilities of the Internet—those capabilities provided by only the most professional Web sites in cyberspace. With these skills, you can improve your piece of the Web to compete with the best that technology can offer.

Chapter 3

VB Script, Literals, and Variables

DATA? INFORMATION? WHAT IS IT?

Now that you have a good understanding of standard HTML and how markup tags are used to direct the browser to display your creation to the thousands cyberspacenauts who will visit your Web site, it is time to cook up some magic to dazzle the new visitors. Your magic potion is a mixture of information and words used to have the computer manipulate the data. Your magic potion is the VB Script language.

With this chapter, you begin learning how to use these words to harness the potential of cyberspace. We start with a close look at a fundamental building block of every computer application—information. The purpose of a computer application is to do something with information. The technical term for pieces of information is *data*.

Say that you want each visitor to your Web site to log in and be granted permission to use your cyberspace facility. Technically, your application displays information on the screen—an instruction to log in—and then collects information from the visitor. This data is then processed by the application and new information is sent to the visitor—the message that he or she has successfully logged into the Web site. How does the VB Script application manage this information? By now you realize it isn't with magic.

Web Data

All information used by your Web site is in the form of the electronic equivalent of ones and zeros, the binary values. We really don't care too much about them, except when it comes to representing the characters that make up the data we use in our Web site. Each character that appears in the HTML file is composed of a combination of eight ones and zeros called a *byte*. For example, a capital *A* is really a specific combination of eight ones and zeros.

Fortunately, as Web site developers, we don't have to worry about this because our text editors and browsers interpret the binary values into characters on the screen for us. Why even bring up this issue? You will use this knowledge when you prepare your VB Script to handle information for your Web page.

However, before moving ahead we need to understand how data is stored by the computer in memory. Consider computer memory as a series of cells, with each cell able to hold one byte of information. Does that sound familiar? It should, since one of the questions asked when you purchased your computer probably was, "How many bytes of memory do you want?" Now you know one reason for asking that question. Each character is a byte and, therefore, requires one byte of memory to hold it while your VB Script program manipulates this information.

Information used on your Web page is called data. Data can take many forms, such as a single character to represent the order of an item in an ordered list or many characters, such as in the description of that item. As you can imagine, the amount of data used by your Web page can fluctuate both as you begin to construct the page and while the page is being used by a visitor to your Web site.

When someone first connects to your Web site, the browser transfers a copy of your index.html file to the visitor's computer. This file contains information (data) in the form of text and markup tags, which is then placed into bytes of memory on the visitor's computer and remains there until it is released by the browser or the computer is turned off.

Typically, the index.html file directs the browser to load an image file, such as a logo. This file also contains bytes of data and is brought into the computer's memory before the image is displayed on the screen. Additional data must be reserved by the browser if your HTML file contains the <INPUT> markup tag. This instructs the browser to read information from the keyboard into memory. Therefore, the browser must be sure sufficient memory is available to store the maximum number of characters specified by the MAXLENGTH attribute.

Avoid Congestion on the Superhighway

Consider a byte to be like a car and the Internet like a highway—a super electronic highway. When a browser requests a file from your Web site, it's like all the workers of an industrial plant hitting the highway at the same time. The more workers in the plant, the more cars will be in the parking lot or traveling on the highway at the same time. This is a formula for congestion.

On the Internet superhighway, all the bytes in the requested file must take the superhighway for the trip to the visitor's computer. The greater the number of bytes in the file and in other files traveling the highway at the same time as yours, the longer it will take for the visitor to view the file on the screen.

You've probably experienced a delay displaying information during peak times on the Internet. This is due to congestion on the superhighway. The solution? Well, no can remove this congestion. However, you can help matters along by keeping the size of your Web files small. You'll find better performance by having small amounts of data in several files than having the same amount of information in one file.

Web Data That Doesn't Change

The information we are talking about is data that doesn't change in memory, called a *literal*. A literal consists of the literal bytes that represent a character. All the characters that compose your Web page are literals. For example, the <H1> markup tag is a piece of information whose value is not changed while the visitor is reading your Web page.

Other literals in a typical Web page are values assigned to attributes. You'll recall that the attribute VALUE is used to set the default value for the <INPUT> markup tag. This is the value that is used by the browser if the visitor does not enter information. The value assigned to the VALUE attribute consists of character(s) contained within double quotation marks. These characters are literals and will not change their value during the life of the Web page.

Life? A literal doesn't breathe or have a heartbeat. How can it have a life? Each piece of data has a life cycle just like us. Data is born when the information is placed in computer memory, where it lives until the data is killed when the browser removes the data from memory. Data has the same life as the life of the file that contains the data.

Placing a VB Script into Your Web Page

A VB Script is actually embedded into a Web page, not in a separate file as in other programming languages. The VB Script is identified to the browser by using the <SCRIPT> and </SCRIPT> markup tags. Within these tags are the statements that form the script.

Browsers do not know how to interpret a VB Script—or a Java Script, for that matter. When the browser sees the <SCRIPT> markup tag, the browser knows it is in trouble. So the browser calls for help from another program called an *engine*. This is the VB Script engine that Microsoft supplied to the browser manufacturer.

Actually, several engines are available to a browser, as long as the browser supports all those engines. The browser knows which engine to use by looking at the value that is assigned to the LANGUAGE attribute. In our case, the value is "VBS."

For example, data in the index.html file remains accessible—lives—until the browser replaces the index.html file in memory with another file from your Web site or from another Web site.

Web Data That Changes

Our discussion about information being literal can seem nothing more than technical bantering with little effect on tapping into the magic offered by VB Script. Well, there's more to data than literals. As you are probably thinking, if there is information that doesn't change, then there must be information that changes. And you're correct.

Data that changes during the life of the Web page file is assigned to temporary locations in memory. Each byte of memory is identified inside the computer by an address, a memory address. Consider the address of memory as an address of a building in your town. Each car (byte) that travels over the superhighway to your visitor's town (computer) is stored in a building (a unique memory address).

Literals are stored in their own driveways (memory address). Data that change, however, are stored in a parking lot (a temporary address). When the browser is finished using the data, the information will be discarded and the parking space (a temporary address) can be used by another piece of information.

A Web page developer is not concerned about the addresses assigned to literals, since other information will not be stored at that address. However, the developer must be knowledgeable about memory addresses used to store information that will change. Furthermore, the browser must be told to reserve enough space in memory to hold this changing data.

Don't worry about trying to remember strange-looking numbers that represent memory addresses. The computer will handle that. Instead, we can give a memory address an alias—an English name that represents the data that is stored in the location. Such an alias is called a *variable*.

The VB Script engine must be told to reserve memory for a variable before the variable is used in the VB Script. Memory is reserved by using the Dim keyword followed by the name of the variable.

Once your VB Script directs the VB Script engine to reserve memory called defining a variable, a value can be assigned to the memory location by using the equal (=) operator. The value that is assigned the variable, in many cases, is itself a literal. Example 3.1 illustrates these techniques.

Example 3.1 Reserving Space for a Variable

```
<SCRIPT LANGUAGE="VBS">
Dim FirstName
Dim MiddleName, LastName
Let FirstName = "Mary"
MiddleName="Anne"
LastName="Smith"
</SCRIPT>
```

The first two lines of this example define variables. On the first line, a single variable, FirstName, is defined. However, as illustrated on the second line, multiple variables can be defined on the same line by separating each variable name with a comma. After these lines are read by the VB Script engine, it reserves space in the computer's memory for each variable.

The third and fourth lines of this VB Script place data into memory at the corresponding address. This is called assigning a value to a variable. On line 3, the Let keyword is used for the assignment. This is a throwback to the early days of the BASIC language. Today, you have the option of using the keyword or, as shown in the fourth line, simply disregarding this keyword. Both lines assign values to variables.

Values that are assigned to a variable fall into two general categories: strings and numbers. A *string* is a literal that consists of one or more characters placed within quotation marks. A *number* is a literal that is a numeric value that can be used in mathematical manipulations such as arithmetic.

Example 3.1 illustrates the technique of assigning strings to a variable. A number can be assigned to a variable using the same method except that the number is not enclosed in quotation marks.

Once a value is placed into memory by assigning the value to a previously defined variable, the name of the variable can be used throughout the VB Script whenever there is a need to use the value assigned to the variable. Furthermore, a different value can be assigned to the same variable elsewhere in the VB Script.

Example 3.2 shows how variables can be reassigned a different value. When this occurs, the new value replaces the old value in memory. That is, the old value is destroyed and cannot be recovered.

Example 3.2 Reassigning a Value to a Variable

```
<SCRIPT LANGUAGE="VBS">
Dim FirstName
Dim MiddleName, LastName
Let FirstName = "Mary"
MiddleName="Anne"
LastName="Smith"
FirstName = "Joe"
MiddleName="Bob"
LastName="Jones"
</SCRIPT>
```

Although the previous examples assigned a literal to a variable, the value of another variable can be assigned to a variable as well. Remember, once a variable is assigned a value, you can use the name of the variable as if you were using the value itself. This is shown in Example 3.3, where three variables are defined, then two are assigned numeric values. Notice, on the fourth line of the VB Script, that the *total* variable is assigned the sum of the other two variables.

Example 3.3 Assigning the Value of a Variable to Another Variable

```
<SCRIPT LANGUAGE="VBS">
Dim val1, val2, total
val1= 5
val2= 10
total= val1 + val2
</SCRIPT>
```

WHAT'S IN A NAME

The trick of placing data into memory wasn't hard to learn: Define a variable, give it a name, then assign it a value. Hold on! Don't minimize the importance of naming the variable. Giving a variable an improper name will make your VB Script confusing to read—and it may not work at all.

A variable is an alias, a shorthand method of symbolizing the actual address inside the computer, which none of us ever wants to know personally. The alias is also a symbol for the information stored at the memory address. Therefore, it is up to you to make sure that the alias—the variable name—gives you an indication of the type of information contained in that address.

Various styles can be used to convey the meaning of the data through the name of the variable. In Examples 3.1 and 3.2, the names of the variables reflect the values assigned to them. In addition, these names use a choice of upper or lowercase letters to make it easier for anyone to read the individual words that make up the variable name.

Another technique that achieves the same results is to separate these words with an underscore, such as first_name, middle_name, and last_name. Practically any combination of letters that infers the kind of data assigned to the variable is an acceptable style.

Microsoft suggests another variable naming style. This third style includes the data type of the information as a prefix to the name of the variable. Table 3.1 contains a listing of this style. Notice that the prefix *str* is used as part of the name of a variable that is assigned to a string. This informs anyone who reads the name of the variable that the data represented by the variable name is a string. Example 3.4 is similar to the previous examples except that variable names conform to the Microsoft style of naming variables.

Table 3.1 Microsoft Recommended Naming Convention for Variables

Type of Data	*Suggested Prefix*	*Sample Name*
Boolean	bln	blnFound
Byte	byt	bytRasterData
Date (time)	dtm	dtmStart
Double	dbl	dblTolerance
Error	err	errOrderNum
Integer	int	intQuantity
Long	lng	lngDistance
Single	sng	sngAverage
String	str	strFirstName

Example 3.4 Naming Variables in the Microsoft Style

```
<SCRIPT LANGUAGE="VBS">
Dim strFirstName
Dim strMiddleName, strLastName
strFirstName = "Mary"
strMiddleName="Anne"
strLastName="Smith"
</SCRIPT>
```

Data type? What's a data type? A *data type* is a technical description of how much memory is required to store data and how the VB Script engine is to manipulate the data. We'll discuss this concept in detail later in this chapter.

Keep in mind that whatever naming style you adopt for your VB Script, it is up to you to maintain the style. That is, neither the VB Script engine nor the browser cares what naming conventions are used in a VB Script. For example, you can call a variable strLastName, then assign a numeric value to the variable. This will obviously be misleading to anyone who reads the VB Script but it is totally acceptable to the VB Script engine and the browser.

However, even the VB Script engine won't accept some naming conventions. A variable name must begin with an alphabetic character and cannot contain an embedded period anywhere in the name. No more than 255 characters can be used to form the variable name. And the variable name must be unique within the scope in which the variable is declared.

WHO HAS THE SCOPE?

The scope has nothing to do with mouthwash or submarines. *Scope* is the segment of the VB Script that can access a variable. Sound confusing? It might, since we can easily assume that a variable can be used anywhere in a VB Script, as is the case in the examples shown so far in this chapter. However, when we look at the parts of a VB Script the importance of the scope of a variable becomes apparent. Complex VB Scripts are divided into two levels. The top level is called the *script level*. All the examples presented in this chapter are at the script level. The level below the script level is called the *procedure level*.

A *procedure* is a group of VB Script statements that are treated as a group. The unit is given a unique name. The statements contained in a procedure are executed by specifying the procedure name in the VB Script.

Think of a procedure as your assistant. You can ask your assistant to perform specific tasks, such as "Bring me my magic hat." Note that you don't tell your assistant how to perform this task, just that you want the task performed at this period of time during your magic act. Your assistant knows how to perform this task.

We'll spend a whole chapter showing you how to create and work with procedures. For now, however, let's be concerned with how the scope of a variable is affected by a procedure. A variable that is defined within a procedure can be used only within that procedure. VB Script statements at the script level cannot use those variables.

Back to the assistant for a moment. When setting out to find your magic hat, your assistant probably refers to a note he or she made, telling where the hat is located. Doesn't the notepad remind you of a variable, and the message written on the notepad, the data assigned to the variable? The information on the notepad is only important for the assistant to know, not for you. After all, you don't care where the magic hat is located.

In contrast, a variable created at the script level is available to the entire VB Script, including all the procedures called by the script. This is like you having a notepad with the location of the magic hat on your table. Both you and your assistant have access to the notepad.

Variables defined within a procedure are called *local variables*, since they are local—accessible only to VB Script statements contained within that procedure. Variables defined on the script level are called *global variables*, because their scope encompasses the entire script.

When a variable goes out of scope, it dies. The value assigned to the variable no longer exists in memory. In fact, the memory location that contained the variable becomes available to be used again by a different variable. A global variable is alive until the VB Script stops running. When the script is rerun, the global variable must be redefined and reassigned a value.

A similar concept is true with local variables. A local variable is alive only during the execution of the procedure. Once the procedures ends, so does the life of the variable. Each time the procedure is called, the variable must be defined anew and assigned a value.

So when you perform your bit of VB Script magic, should you use global or local variables? As a general rule, variables should have a limited scope. In other words, local variables are preferred over global variables because this reduces the amount of memory required by your VB Script. Remember, global variables take up memory throughout the life of the script, while memory used for local variables is freed when the variable goes out of scope.

WHAT TYPE OF DATA IS IT, ANYWAY?

Who cares! Well, that's not totally an accurate reply. We said that information can be stored in memory if the VB Script reserved sufficient memory to hold the data. Information that consists of a single character requires a single byte. However, information that is a numeric value may require two or more bytes. And information that is either true or false—a Boolean value—requires one-eighth of a byte, called a *bit*.

Bytes, bits—is this necessary? Fortunately, the answer is no when you are dealing with VB Script. This is not necessarily the case in other programming languages, however. Typically, in other programming languages, the programmer is required to specify the data type of a variable when the variable is defined in the program by using a keyword.

Microsoft removed this requirement when defining variables in VB Script. VB Script has one data type, which is called a *variant*. This is a new data type to any programmer reading this book. However, you'll quickly embrace the idea of a variant data type. The magic in a variant data type is that the VB Script engine manipulates a variant based on the kind of data that is assigned to the variable.

If the value assigned to a variable is contained within quotation marks, then the VB Script engine assumes the information is a string and treats the variable as if the programmer defined the variable as a string data type. Likewise, if a variable is assigned a numeric value in the range of –32,768 to 32,767, the VB Script engine assumes the data is an integer data type and handles it accordingly.

You don't have to worry about the data type of a variable or telling the VB Script engine to reserve sufficient memory for the information contained in your script. All this work is performed by the VB Script engine, behind the scenes.

Although VB Script has a single data type called a variant, VB Script does contain subtypes. A *subtype* is what programmers commonly know as data types. Table 3.2 contains a list of the subtypes. When you assign one of these values to a variable to place the variable, the VB Script engine recognizes the variable as having a corresponding subtype. Don't become overly concerned about subtypes. Simply define a variable within your VB Script, then assign a value to the variable; the VB Script engine will handle any issues about data type.

Table 3.2 VB Script Data Type Subtypes

Subtype	*Description*
Boolean	Contains either true or false
Byte	Contains an integer in the range 0 to 255
Integer	Contains an integer in the range –32,768 to 32,767
Long	Contains an integer in the range –2,147,483,648 to 2,147,483,647
Single	Contains a single-precision, floating-point number in the range –3.402823E38 to –1.401298E–45 for negative values and 1.401298E–45 to 3.402823E38 forpositive values
Double	Contains a double-precision, floating-point number in the range –1.79769313486232E308 to –4.94065645841247E–324 for negative values and 4.94065645841247E–324 to 1.79769313486232E308 for positive values
Date (time)	Contains a number that represents a date between January 1, 100 to December 31, 9999
String	Contains a variable-length string that can be up to approximately 2 billion characters in length
Error	Contains an error number

MIXING IT UP WITH WEB DATA

Now that you have some idea of variables and data types, we'll show you how to perform a little magic with Web data. Although you need not be concerned with data types when defining a variable, you do have to be alert to ensure that your VB Script manipulates the variables properly.

Example 3.5 illustrates this point. Three variables are defined, all of the variant data type. Next, one of those variables, strSalary, is assigned to what appears to be numeric data contained within quotation marks. We know from our discussion earlier in this chapter that the subtype of this variable is a string (quotation marks surround the numeric characters).

On the next line another variable, intBonus, is assigned a value that is the numeric value 200. Notice that this value is not enclosed within quotation marks. This means that the VB Script engine will treat this variable as an integer subtype.

On the last line of the script, both variables are added together, with the sum assigned to the intTotalComp variable. How can the VB Script engine add together values of unlike subtypes? Simply put, the VB Script engine cannot add a string data type value to an integer data type value. It just won't come up with the expected results. This illustrates why it is important that you keep track of the subtype of every variable used in an expression. (Expression? That's covered in the next chapter.)

Example 3.5 Conflicting Subtype Variables

```
<SCRIPT LANGUAGE="VBS">
Dim strSalary
Dim intBonus, intTotalComp
strSalary="10000"
intBonus=200
intTotalComp = strSalary + intBonus
</SCRIPT>
```

Fortunately, VB Script contains a method of working with unlike subtype variables in an expression such as the calculation shown in Example 3.5. VB Script's solution is to let the VB Script engine perform some more magic for you. All you need to do is call one of several functions that are built into VB Script.

A *function* is a segment of a VB Script that Microsoft built in to perform some of the more complex data manipulations (actually this is an oversimplification but it will suffice). Consider them tricks you can add to your VB Script magic kit. All you need to know to use a function is the name of the function and the information that the function requires to perform its magic.

Example 3.6 solves the mixed subtype problem of Example 3.5 by calling the CInt() function to convert the string value to an integer value. Once the conversion has taken place, the VB Script engine can add the values and assign the results to the intTotalComp variable.

Example 3.6 Converting a String Subtype to an Integer Subtype

```
<SCRIPT LANGUAGE="VBS">
Dim strSalary
Dim intBonus, intTotalComp
strSalary="10000"
intBonus=200
intTotalComp = CInt(strSalary) + intBonus
</SCRIPT>
```

Notice that the CInt() function requires information before it can perform its magic. The function needs to know the name—or the literal—that contains the string subtype. This information is placed between the parentheses of the function. Functions have a secret. They return a value to VB Script. The value is normally used in an expression. In this example, the return value is the integer version of the value of strSalary and is used in the expression that sums two integer values. Table 3.3 contains functions that can be used to convert values of one subtype variable to another subtype.

Table 3.3 VB Script Subtype Conversion Functions

Function	*Converts to Subtype*
CBool(expression)	Boolean
CByte(expression)	Byte
CDbl(expression)	Double
CInt(expression)	Integer
CLng(expression)	Long
CSng(expression)	Single
CStr(expression)	String

Chapter 4

Express Yourself with Expressions, Operators, and Statements

Some More VB Script Tricks Coming Your Way

So you can save information into memory, big deal! Actually, you know how to instruct the VB Script engine to save the data into memory, but who's going to quibble about this detail? Saving information to memory doesn't do anything to dazzle your Web site visitors. You must *do* something with this information. And that's the magic you'll learn in this chapter.

Doing something with the information—really, directing the VB Script engine to perform the task—requires more thought than simply typing on the computer keyboard. Remember, you are the actual brains of the computer. The computer itself is dumb and can only follow your explicit directions on how to do the magic trick.

You may say that you don't know how to do it yourself, so how can you teach the computer? You *do* know these tricks. Say that you want the computer to calculate the total compensation that you received from your job. The computer doesn't know how to do this but you do, by adding together your salary and bonus—if you were lucky enough to receive a bonus.

You still may think that you don't know how to teach the computer this trick. Think again. The computer learns to perform a task by following the instructions that are placed within a VB Script, some of the same instructions you learned in the previous chapter. In fact, the complete set of instructions necessary for the computer to calculate total compensation was presented in the previous chapter. So, you are beginning to acquire these magical skills.

In this chapter, you'll expand those VB Script skills and learn how to interpret a solution to a real-life problem into terms the computer can understand and, therefore, can help you solve.

LET'S DO SOME THINKING BEFORE WE WRITE OUR VB SCRIPT

Writing a VB Script in many cases is the easiest piece of the solution. The hardest part is to understand the problem in sufficient detail to formulate a solution. In whiz kid terminology, this formula is called an *algorithm*—a way of doing something; in this case, solving the problem. At first glance you may think this is a trivial process, since you solve problems every day. However, try your hand at writing instructions.

Assume you have a partner who knows nothing. Write the instructions for your partner to draw three objects on a piece of paper using a pencil: a circle, square, and triangle. Remember, your partner does not know these objects by name so you'll have to be very detailed in your instructions (hint: connect the dots). I'm being a stickler for detail, but then remember your partner doesn't know what paper or a pencil is.

Too easy for you? All right, then write down step-by-step instructions to have your partner put on a sweater. Your partner still knows nothing.

Computer science students have spent days trying to write these same instructions without much success. These simple, everyday tasks that we take for granted become insurmountable obstacles when we are forced to create specific instructions to perform these tasks. This is the job that you undertake every time that you try to dazzle your Web site visitors when you create a VB Script or any program.

Where do you begin? First, don't panic. Approach the problem logically. If you can perform a task, so can your Web site by following your proper instructions written using VB Script. Establish a clear objective for the VB Script. Return to Examples 3.5 and 3.6, where the VB Script determined the total compensation for an individual. Be patient. We'll get into more interesting examples after you learn more about VB Script. For now we'll stay with a simple example to learn how to build an expression.

Once the objective is set, you must determine the steps necessary to reach this objective. List these steps in order of performance, as shown in Table 4.1. Too detailed? You need to be very detailed when you instruct the VB Script engine to perform any magic on your Web page. So get used to thinking about the finer points of solving your problems.

Writing Down Your Thoughts

The steps that you've outlined to solve your problem should be entered directly into your VB Script as comments. Lines that begin with an exclamation point (!) are ignored by the VB Script engine and, therefore,

Table 4.1 Steps Necessary to Calculate Total Compensation

Determine the values that are necessary to calculate total compensation.
Reserve space in memory for these values.
Place the values in memory.
Determine the calculation that is necessary to arrive at the total compensation amount.
Describe the calculation in a way that the VB Script engine will understand.

are suitable for entering as comments into your script. This is illustrated in Example 4.1.

Example 4.1 Using the Steps Necessary to Solve a Problem as the Outline for Your Script

```
<SCRIPT LANGUAGE="VBS">
! Determine the values necessary to calculate total compensation.

! Reserve space in memory for these values.

! Place the values in memory.

! Determine the calculation that is necessary to arrive at the total
compensation amount.

! Describe the calculation in a way that the VB Script engine will
understand.

</SCRIPT>
```

Now you can expand this outline by adding lines that translate your requirements into the VB Script language. Beneath the first comment line in the outline, you can add another comment that lists the two pieces of information necessary for the calculation: salary and bonus. This information can be used as a notation for you or anyone else who reads your VB Script.

The next step in the outline is to reserve space in memory for this data. Remember how to do this? Use the Dim keyword followed by the name of the variable. Then you must place values in memory. Hmm, that's something you've done before. Use the variable name, the equal operator, and the numeric value.

Our outline calls for you to describe the method you'll use to determine the total compensation value. This is a notation and, therefore, is written as a comment in the VB Script. Example 4.2 incorporates these changes into the previous example. Hold on! Isn't a piece missing from the script? Yes, and we'll tackle that in the next section of this chapter.

Example 4.2 Translating Your Solution into the VB Script Language

```
<SCRIPT LANGUAGE="VBS">
! Determine the values necessary to calculate total compensation.
! salary and bonus

! Reserve space in memory for these values.
Dim intSalary, intBonus, intTotalComp

! Place the values in memory.
intSalary = 10000
intBonus = 300

! Determine the calculation necessary to arrive at the total compensation
amount.

! Add the salary and the bonus to arrive at the total compensation value.

! Describe the calculation in a way that the VB Script engine will understand.

</SCRIPT>
```

Nothing Is Secret on Your Web Page

Whenever you devise a brilliant trick for your Web page, don't expect to keep your technique secret. Remember, a Web page is basically a plain word processing file (text file), which contains special codes that can be read by any visitor with a browser. Your Web page is electronically copied to the visitor's computer and the browser can be used to save your Web page file to the visitor's disk.

Once your Web page is on the visitor's disk, he or she can use any editor, such as Notepad, to view your Web page and see your text, markup tags, and the contents of your VB Script. Your secret is out. The illusion is blown.

There is really no secret about your Web page unless your Web script uses a language that is compiled into binary code, which only the best hackers can read. Java is one of those compiled languages. JavaScript and VB Script are interpretive languages and are not compiled.

THE DANCING WEB DATA

Now the real magic begins. You translate your wishes into magic words that direct the VB Script engine to manipulate data stored in memory. Data manipulation sounds like something you'd need a degree from MIT to understand. Not so—you already know how to manipulate data. You do it every day when you perform arithmetic.

Data manipulation is little more than using information to create or change other information. In addition, two values are mathematically combined to create a new value, the sum of the other two values. However, the trick is to have the VB Script engine manipulate data for you.

This is a trick, you may think, since the VB Script engine does not understand English. Of course not, but the VB Script engine does understand the VB Script language, which you are learning in this book. Once you are comfortable using the VB Script language, you'll find that giving orders to the VB Script engine will become a subconscious exercise.

The VB Script language is closer to the English language than you might realize. In English we converse by assembling words into expressions. The same is true in the VB Script language. The words are called *keywords* and the expressions are called . . . *expressions*. We form expressions in the VB Script language by connecting keywords of the language.

Actually, it is a little more complicated than that, but not too much more. The components of a VB Script expression are called operands and operators. An *operand* is data or another expression that is acted on by an operator. An *operator* is like a verb, in that it tells the VB Script engine how to manipulate the operand.

An operand can take the form of literal data, such as a character or a numeric value, and can also be the name of a variable. Likewise, the result of another expression can be used as an operand.

Operands? Let's cut the high tech talk and get down to something everyone can understand. Take a look at Example 4.3, especially at the line that sums salary and bonus amounts (intTotalComp = intSalary + intBonus). This line is an expression. The operands are intTotalComp, intSalary, and intBonus. The operators are the equal sign (=) and the plus sign (+). This should clear up any confusion about operands and operators.

Example 4.3 Operands and Operators

```
<SCRIPT LANGUAGE="VBS">
Dim intSalary, intBonus, intTotalComp
intSalary=10000
intBonus=200
intTotalComp = intSalary + intBonus
</SCRIPT>
```

There actually are two other expressions in this VB Script. These are on the second and third lines, where values are assigned to variables. Here, the variable names and the literal values are the operands and the equal sign (=) is the operator.

Expressions are read in a very systematic way by the VB Script engine. Each expression is read left to right, with some exceptions that will be covered later on in this chapter. Let's take a closer look at the first expression (intSalary=10000) to see what we are telling the VB Script engine to perform.

This expression states the following: Take the value 10000 and store it in the memory address that is associated with the variable intSalary. The equal sign is the key to this whole process. It directs the VB Script engine to take the value of the operand to the immediate right of the equal sign and copy the value to the operand on the immediate left of the equal sign.

Obvious, you may be thinking. However, it is important that you have a firm understanding of how the VB Script engine reads an expression. Expressions can become very complex, very quickly. A poorly constructed expression will produce undesirable results, as we'll see later in this chapter.

We looked at how a simple expression is read by the VB Script engine. The technical way to say this is "evaluated by the VB Script engine." Now let's follow the same process to see how a more complex expression is evaluated. We'll explore the last line in the VB Script: intTotalComp = intSalary + intBonus.

The first set of operands and operators evaluated is intSalary + intBonus In English this means "combine the operand on the right of the plus sign operator with the operand on the left of the plus sign."

Next, the remaining portion of the expression is evaluated: intTotalComp =. Note that there seems to be one operand and one operator—but the equal operator requires two operands. The second operand is the result of the evaluation of the first part of the expression, which is the sum of intSalary and intBonus. The sum is copied to the operand on the left of the equal operator. Now you're beginning to speak the VB Script language and you can probably complete the VB Script shown in Example 4.2

No, I Go First! I Go First!

We said that the VB Script engine follows the left-to-right rule. Actually, this rule applies to how the operators manipulate operands. The operator takes the operand on the right and does something. The task it performs depends on the type of operator used. However, a problem can arise when many operators are used in an expression. Recall that two operators are used in Example 4.3: the equal operator and the plus operator.

Imagine an expression that contains three or four operators or an expression that contains other expressions. These will be discussed in later chapters. Not only can you become confused over the order in which these operators will be called by the VB Script engine, so can the VB Script engine.

As you can guess, another trick clears the smoke from this confusion. This is called the *order of precedence*. Table 4.2 illustrates the order in a

Table 4.2 The Precedence Table

Arithmetic	*Comparison*	*Logical*
Exponentiation (^)	Equality (=)	NOT
Negation (–)	Inequality (<>)	AND
Multiplication and division (*, /)	Less than (<)	OR
Integer division (\)	Greater than (>)	XOR
Module arithmetic (Mod)	Less than or equal to (<=)	EQV
Addition and subtraction (+, –)	Greater than or equal to (>=)	IMP
String concatenation (&)	Like	IS

NOTE: When expressions contain operators from more than one category, the order of precedence is arithmetic operator, comparison operator, then logical operator.

precedence table, showing the order in which the VB Script engine will evaluate operators in an expression.

Confused? All right, try to solve the simple expression shown in Example 4.4. Does the value of *total* equal 40 or 80? There's a big difference and only one answer is correct, although both can be derived from the expression.

Example 4.4 What is the Value of *total*?

```
total = 10 + 6 * 5
```

The trick is to know if you perform the addition or multiplication first. How do you know which operation is performed first by the VB Script engine? You consult the precedence table. If you look at Table 4.2, you'll notice that multiplication has a higher precedence than addition; therefore, multiplication is performed before addition in this expression.

Still confused? Do you really have to memorize the complete table to create a VB Script expression? No, most VB Script programmers take one of two approaches to solving this problem. The first approach is to keep expressions simple. Then, when it is necessary to create a complex expression, refer to the precedence table.

The second approach, however, is much clearer. Create a complex expression if it is required to solve a problem, then use parentheses to break up the expression into components that are smaller expressions. The VB Script engine disregards the precedence table whenever it comes across parentheses in an expression and evaluates the piece of the expression that appears within the parentheses first.

Note that parentheses are used in Example 4.5 to remove the confusion that appeared in the same expression in Example 4.4. The VB Script engine performs the addition and then the multiplication on the first line because of the placement of the parentheses. The reverse evaluation is performed on the second line, although the parentheses are not required since this follows the normal order of precedence.

Example 4.5 Clarifying a Complex Expression

```
total = (10 + 6) * 5
total = 10 (6 * 5)
```

Embedding parentheses in an expression explicitly tells the VB Script engine in what order you want the expression to be evaluated by the VB Script engine. This same technique also clarifies the evaluation process to anyone reading the expression, without requiring that person to review the precedence table.

ARITHMETIC, COMPARISON, OR LOGICAL? SIMPLY MAGIC!

To write a VB Script to solve a problem, outline the steps necessary to resolve the problem, then interpret each step into an appropriate statement that is recognized by the VB Script engine. When a step requires the manipulation of information, you need an expression that tells the VB Script engine how to manipulate the data.

In the previous section, we explored how to use a few operators that function similar to the way the same operators work in arithmetic. VB Script offers a variety of operators that perform arithmetic operations, comparison operations, and logical operations. Although you probably have a good idea of what arithmetic operations are, comparison and logical operations might be a puzzle. We'll solve this puzzle.

A *comparison operator* asks the VB Script engine to determine if operands—data—are the same. Does the password entered at the keyboard match the password on file? The VB Script programmer must formulate an expression using the proper operand and comparison operator to have the VB Script engine answer this question. Sometimes a comparison operator is called a *pattern matching operator,* since the operator compares data character by character, and the data can be of any type.

Another kind of operator used to formulate VB Script expressions is the logical operator. A *logical operator* is used to manipulate operands that are either true or false values. Confused again? Let's take a step backwards. Expressions that use a comparison operator ask a question, the answer of which is either "true" or "false"—nothing else. For example, is the password entered at the keyboard the same as the password on file? The answer is "true" (or "false").

However, we know that when someone logs into a computer system, two questions are asked: Are the user identification and the password the same as are on file? A bit of VB Script language magic must be woven to answer these questions, but you know this trick. Each question is an expression (strUID="Mary" strPassword="Pass").

Now the trick is to combine these two expressions to properly ask the VB Script engine to find out the answer for you. In comes the logical operator, in this case, the AND logical operator, which will be discussed later in this chapter.

We said that a logical operator manipulates only operands that have a logical value of true or false. When these expressions are combined using a logical operator, the result of each expression (true or false) becomes an operand for the logical operator. Hold on if you're still cloudy over this concept. The sun will burn away the clouds a little later in this chapter.

Just a Matter of Those Magic Numbers

No, you're not going to be taught arithmetic.Your knowledge of arithmetic is the same skill that you need to create arithmetic expressions that use the arithmetic operators. However, a few arithmetic operators are not intuitive.

For example, two arithmetic operators are used for division: the forward slash (/) operator and the backward slash (\) operator. The *forward slash operator* instructs the VB Script engine to divide two operands and return a result as a floating-point number, that is, a decimal value. In comparison, the *backward slash operator* performs a similar function except the result is rounded to an integer value. Another division operator is the *modulus operator,* which returns the fractional portion of the resulting value. For example, 5 divided by 2 results in the value 2.5. If the modulus operator is used (result = 5 MOD 2) then 0.5 is the result of this expression.

Another operator that can be confusing is the exponent (^) operator. The *exponent operator* is used to raise a value by a specified power. Say you want to multiply 5 * 5. This is the same as saying raise the value 5 by the power of 2, or 5 squared. In the VB Script language, the exponent operator is used in the expression: 5^2. Likewise, 5 * 5 * 5 is the same as raising 5 to the power of 3, or 5^3 or 5 cubed.

VB Script contains a special kind of addition called *string concatenation* that uses the string concatenation (&) operator. Remember, a string is a subtype data of one or more characters that are grouped using quotation marks. Two strings can be joined together by using the concatenation operator.

This technique is illustrated in Example 4.6. Here, three string variables are defined and two of them assigned string values, the first and last name of a person. The last line in the script combines these names and assigns the combination to the variable strFullName. Just a note: You can also use the plus operator (+) to perform the same task; however, Microsoft recommends the use of the concatenation operator for clarity.

Example 4.6 Using the String Concatenation Operator

```
<SCRIPT LANGUAGE="VBS">
Dim strFirstName, strLastName, strFullName
strFirstName="Mary"
strLastName="Smith"
strFullName=strFirstName & strLastName
</SCRIPT>
```

Looks the Same to Me

Whenever two pieces of information need to be compared, you must use a comparison operator. The VB Script language offers the typical comparison operators found in mathematics and other programming languages. For example, when you want to have the VB Script engine determine if two operands are the same value, you can use the equality (=) operator (a = b). A "true" value is returned if both are of equal value, otherwise a "false" is returned.

However, if your program needs to know if the values of two operands are not equal, then the inequality operator (<>) is used in your expression, such as (a <> b). A "true" value is returned if the values are not the same; otherwise, a "false" value is returned.

Both the equality and inequality operators provide a black and white test. Both values are the same or they are not the same. However, there will be occasions when you need to test the range of values rather than a specific value. Is the value of A greater than the value of B? Is the value of A less than the value of B? Is the value of A less than or equal to the value of B? Is the value of A greater than or equal to the value of B? These questions are answered by formulating a VB Script expression that uses the less than (<), greater than (>), less than or equal to (<=), and greater than or equal to (>=) operators. The proper use of these operators is shown in Table 4.3.

Table 4.3 The Comparison Operators

A = B	A is equal to B
A <> B	A is not equal to B
A < B	A is less than B
A > B	A is greater than B
A <= B	A is less than or equal to B
A >= B	A is greater than or equal to B

True and False

Well, here's some more techno jargon sure to confuse any Web site magician. When the VB Script engine is asked to compare operands or evaluate a logical expression, it returns a value—a number. Actually, only two numbers are returned in these situations: –1 or 0.

In techno jargon, 0 refers to a false and –1 is considered a true. So when your script asks the VB Script engine if the value of A is the same as the value of B (A=B), we say the response is either true or false. In the VB Script language this translates to a –1 or 0.

Seems Logical to Me

In the previous section we had the VB Script engine compare two values, then tell you—actually, tell your VB Script—if the values are alike. The response is in the form of a numeric value that represents true or false (see box, below). Comparisons are made within an expression, and sometimes more than one expression is necessary for the VB Script engine to perform the task.

Let's say that, before your script takes a particular action, certain conditions must exist. The script is told to give a salary raise of 10% to those employees of Department 24 who have a salary below $20,000. Example 4.7 illustrates the VB Script language interpretation of these criteria.

Example 4.7 Both Conditions Must Be True

```
strDeptNum="24" AND intSalary < 20000
```

Note that there are two expressions. The first is strDeptNum="24" and the second expression is intSalary < 20000. Each of these expressions uses a comparison operator. However, the results of both comparisons are necessary for the action to be taken. Expressions are combined by using a logical operator.

In this example, the AND logical operator is used to join expressions. A logical operator manipulates operands that contain logical values. A logical value is 0 or a nonzero value such as –1. The logical operands shown here are the results of each expression. Remember, a comparison operator returns a value of 0 or –1.

If strDeptNum is equal to "24", then the equivalent operator returns –1. If intSalary is less than $20,000, then the less than operator returns –1. Both expressions are true. Therefore, the AND operator returns –1, indicating that the combined expressions are true. In contrast, if either expression is not true, then the AND operator returns 0—the combined expressions are false.

Now suppose you decided to give everyone who has a salary of less than $20,000 and everyone who is in Department 24 a raise of 10%. The compound expression in Example 4.7 won't help you isolate the affected employees. In this example, employees making less than $20,000 must work in Department 24 to receive the raise. Those employees who receive less than $20,000 and do *not* work in Department 24 will not receive a 10% raise.

We can use the OR logical operator to modify this example to address the problem properly, as shown in Example 4.8. The OR operator returns a true value if either expression in this complex expression returns a true value. In fact, the OR operator also returns a true value if both expressions are true.

Example 4.8 Either Condition Must Be True

```
strDeptNum="24" OR intSalary < 20000
```

Hang on for another twist in the magic of logic. Let's change this problem. Now you want to record that an employee was paid. The employee could be paid in cash or by check but not both ways. The test of these conditions is shown in VB Script language in Example 4.9. The XOR is a logical operator that functions similar to the OR operator except the XOR operator returns a true value only if one of the operands is true, not both.

Example 4.9 One or the Other but Not Both Must Be True

```
strCash="YES" XOR strCheck="YES"
```

The logical result of any expression that uses the comparison or logical operator can be reversed by using the NOT logical operator. Look at how the NOT operator is used in Example 4.10. This is the same complex expression as shown in Example 4.8 except the NOT operator is used to reverse the logical outcome of the expressions.

Is = an Assignment Operator or Equivalence Operator?

No doubt in the recent examples in this chapter, you've noticed that the equal operator is used to determine the equivalent of two values (strDeptNum="24"). This can be confusing to read, since this is the same operator that is used to assign a value to a variable.

The VB Script engine is not confused, because it looks at the context within which the expression is being used. This will become apparent to you in Chapter 6 when you learn about flow control statements, which use the comparison and logical operators to redirect the flow of the script.

However, you don't have to rely on the context of the expression to tell you which operation is being performed by the equal operator. You can replace the equal operator (=) with the equivalent operator (eqv). Both have the same results when used with a comparison or logical operator (strDeptNum eqv "24").

Example 4.10 Brain Teaser

```
NOT strDeptNum="24" OR  NOT intSalary < 20000
```

Here's how it works. The first expression (strDeptNum="24") returns a true value if both operands have the same value. However, we used the NOT operator (NOT strDeptNum="24"), which reverses this logical operator. If the values are the same, then the true value of the expression is reversed to a false.

The same logic applies to the second expression (NOT intSalary < 20000). For the OR operator to return a true value, either the department number must be other than 24 or the salary must be $20,000 or greater. Still confused? Work out this one with a paper and pencil.

IS IT OR ISN'T IT? THE VB SCRIPT ENGINE KNOWS!

Once you begin to construct complex expressions to be evaluated by the VB Script engine, you'll need to determine the status of information assigned to variables. Say that you want to add two numeric variables. The result will obviously be a numeric value. But what would happen if one of those numeric variables actually contains a character or a string of characters? You'll probably receive disappointing results from the expression.

One way to prevent this from occurring is to ask the VB Script engine to check the type of value assigned to the variable before the expression is evaluated. You can do this by using the IsNumeric() operator, which is illustrated in Example 4.11.

Example 4.11 The IsNumeric() Operator

```
IsNumeric(intSalary)
```

Notice that the variable intSalary is placed within the parentheses of the IsNumeric() operator. A true (–1) is returned if the intSalary variable contains a numeric value; otherwise, a false (0) is returned. Once the script determines that the value of the variable is appropriate, then the VB Script engine can add the two values.

Another problem can occur when the VB Script engine is evaluating an expression. One of the variables of the expression may not have been assigned a value. An unassigned variable is called a *null variable*. The value of a null variable is nothing—and this does not mean a zero.

For example, if the variable intSalary is to be added to intBonus, both must have a numeric value. However, one of them might not contain any value, a null value. This will prevent the VB Script engine from completing the valuation, the addition.

This problem can be avoided by using the IsNull() operator, which asks the VB Script engine to check whether a value is assigned to a variable. If so, then a true is returned; otherwise, a false is returned. Example 4.12 shows how this is done.

Example 4.12 The IsNull() Operator

```
IsNull(intSalary)
```

JUST GIVE ME DIRECTIONS

So far in this chapter, we've explored some magic tricks that will have the VB Script engine manipulate data for you. Well, this isn't all true. We've only talked about ways to formulate expressions using operators and operands. We haven't given the VB Script any instructions as yet, except when arithmetic expressions are used in the script.

You probably noticed that examples of expressions that use comparison and logical operators are not in the format of an embedded VB Script in an HTML file. We didn't use the <SCRIPT> tag and related code because expressions that use these operators are not instructions that the VB Script engine can understand.

An instruction to the VB Script engine must be in the form of a statement. A *statement* tells the VB Script engine to perform a task. For example, Dim intSalary is a statement. It tells the VB Script engine to reserve space in memory and identify that memory location as intSalary. Likewise, the assignment expression intSalary=20000 is also a statement that tells the VB Script engine to do something—place the value 20000 in the memory address intSalary. This statement is also an expression.

However, the expression strDeptNum="24" AND intSalary < 20000 is not a statement. It is an expression that can be evaluated by the VB Script engine, but additional keywords are required to transform this expression into a statement. The additional keywords are shown in Example 4.13

Example 4.13 A Statement Using Comparison and Logical Operators

```
<SCRIPT LANGUAGE="VBS">
<
Dim strDeptNum, intSalary
strDeptNum = "24"
intSalary=20000

If strDeptNum="24" AND intSalary < 20000 Then
    intSalary = intSalary * 1.1

End If
>
</SCRIPT>
```

Some of this program is familiar and parts are new. The first four lines of the program reserve space in memory and assign values to those memory addresses. Both of these are statements. The next line is an If Then statement. The If Then statement uses the expression to determine if the salary should be increased by 10%.

The If Then statement is used to control the flow of the script. This and other flow control statements are covered in detailed in Chapter 6. For now, let's explore this statement so that you can appreciate how the If Then statement interacts with the expressions we've learned in this chapter.

Simply, if the expression is true, then the statement within the If Then statement is evaluated. Otherwise, that statement is not evaluated by the VB Script engine. The expression is a complex expression that contains two component expressions. Both of those must be true for the entire complex expression to be true. This was discussed earlier in this chapter.

WHAT'S NEXT?

You now know about HTML and how to create data in VB Script. You also know how to manipulate that information by creating arithmetic, comparison, and logical expressions and how to formulate simple statements that direct the VB Script engine to perform specific tasks.

Some more magic tricks are in store in the next chapter, where you'll learn how to group these tasks into procedures. Think of a procedure as a small script within a larger script. The larger script can call on specific procedures as they are required. This is very similar to the way your browser calls on the VB Script engine whenever a VB Script is encountered within the HTML file. The VB Script engine is like a procedure to the browser.

Chapter 5

Create Procedures for Your Web Page Using VB Script

Call in the Troops

You learned that one of the magic ingredients to a successful Web site is the browser used by your visitors. The browser is the software that interprets the markup tags you embed in your Web page. If a browser can't understand a markup tag, then it can't help you perform your magic trick.

One reason for the browser becoming the focal point of the World Wide Web is because of the many kinds of computers that can have access to your Web site. So why is this important? The answer isn't obvious, although halfway through this explanation you'll be saying "of course!"

When you purchase software for your computer, do you purchase software for a Mac or for a PC? Does it really matter? Of course. The software you purchased is compiled software. That is, the program converted the source code—something like a script—into code suited for your kind of computer. This is why you must be specific when purchasing software for your computer.

However, positions change when you become a Web site owner. Now your only responsibility is to provide Web page files that conform to the Internet standards (HTML, VB Script, etc.). The responsibility for providing software for the computer accessing the page is transferred from the Web site owner to the visitor, who must ensure that his or her computer has the software necessary to read the formatted HTML and other code (such as VB Script) that is embedded into the HTML file on the Web site.

At first glance, this concept is sound. However, the question remains, Will the browsers be able to perform all the magic tricks that the Web site owners require? The answer is, probably not! But what has evolved is a technique whereby browsers ask for help to perform these special tricks. And as we've see in the previous chapters, this help comes in the form of one or more engines.

An *engine* is software, usually provided by an outside software manufacturer such as Microsoft or Sun Microsystems, that becomes a subscript of the browser software. When the browser doesn't know how to perform a task, the browser calls a subscript—the engine—to handle the job. Actually, the engine is a little more than a subscript.

The idea of having a subscript called to perform a specific task isn't a new concept to programmers. In fact, it is a very old concept that you too can use in your VB Scripts. A subscript—small script—is called a VB Script *procedure*. And like an engine, a procedure helps your VB Script perform redundant, complex tasks. In this chapter you'll learn everything you need to know about VB Script procedures.

PROCEDURES ARE TWO OF A KIND

Two kinds of procedures are available to a VB Script programmer: the standard procedures, usually referred to as a procedure, and function procedures. Both are similar in that they contain one or more statements enclosed within a statement block. The only difference between a procedure and a function procedure is that a function returns a value to the VB Script. Confused? Hang in there, we'll go into the details in a few minutes.

First, let's explore the concept of a procedure before talking more about return values. Take a look at this example. You want the VB Script to calculate your total compensation by adding together your salary and bonus. You saw how this problem is translated into the VB Script language in the last chapter. Now let's see how these same statements can be used within a procedure.

Example 5.1 creates a procedure, CalculateTotalComp(). Note that the Sub and End Sub keywords are used to format the Sub statement, which is used to declare a procedure. The Sub statement requires that a name be assigned to the procedure. The name is used to identify the procedure in the main VB Script whenever you want the procedure to be executed by the VB Script engine.

Example 5.1 Creating a Procedure

```
<SCRIPT LANGUAGE="VBS">
<!--
Sub CalculateTotalComp()
        Dim intSalary, intBonus, intTotalComp
    intSalary=20000
    intBonus=200
    intTotalComp = intSalary + intBonus
End Sub
-->
</SCRIPT>
```

Parentheses? Yes, every procedure name must end with parentheses. The parentheses in this example are empty; however, later in this chapter you will be using the parentheses to send values to the procedure. For now we'll leave these parentheses empty.

The next group of statements is familiar to you. These are the statements used in the previous chapter to calculate the total compensation value. The only difference in these statements is that they are now contained within a procedure.

Why? Because we want to be able to isolate segments of a VB Script into smaller, independent groups so that it is easy to maintain. You won't confuse these statements with other statements in the VB Script.

All procedures must end with the End Sub keyword. This tells the VB Script engine that no more statements are to be evaluated within the procedure. When the End Sub keyword is reached, the VB Script engine

What Is ! - -?

No, it isn't a typo. The exclamation mark (!) tells the browser that everything on the line is a comment and should not be evaluated. The browser simply skips this line altogether. The double hyphens (--) instruct the browser not to display the script on the screen if the browser does not have the VB Script engine available to execute the VB Script.

Why would the browser display the script on the screen? Remember, the browser knows only two kinds of information contained in an HTML file: markup codes and text. Markup codes are not displayed and text is displayed. However, the browser must know how to interpret all the markup codes in the HTML file. If it doesn't recognize the markup code, it could assume that this is text, not a markup code. And a browser would then display the characters on the screen.

Be sure to use these characters in your VB Scripts so that your visitors aren't confused about seeing this strange text flow across their screen in the mix of your Web page.

returns to the line of the VB Script that immediately follows the line that called the procedure. We'll see this in practice a little later in this chapter.

WHERE IS THE MAGIC? THERE'S STILL NOTHING ON THE SCREEN!

Even if you knew how to call the previous procedure in your VB Script, you still don't see anything on the screen. However, we'll fix that with a slight modification to the previous VB Script. The new script is shown in Example 5.2.

Example 5.2 Creating a Procedure That Displays Results on the Screen

```
<SCRIPT LANGUAGE="VBS">
<!--
Sub CalculateTotalComp()
    Dim intSalary, intBonus, intTotalComp
    intSalary=20000
    intBonus=200
    intTotalComp = intSalary + intBonus
    MsgBox "Total Compensation is " & intTotalComp
End Sub
-->
</SCRIPT>
```

This is basically the same as the previous procedure except we've given a glimpse of what is to come in later chapters. We used the MsgBox call to display the results of the calculation on the screen in a message box. When this procedure is called, information will be displayed and you'll know that the procedure worked.

Let's continue with this look into the future. In the real world, programmers avoid assigning values directly to variables within a VB Script. In techno jargon this is called *hard coding* values into a script. A preferred approach is to have the values entered from the keyboard or other data sources. But let's not get too far ahead of ourselves. We'll address the issue of entering data from the keyboard for now.

Example 5.3 uses the InputBox("Enter bonus: ", 1) statement to retrieve information from the keyboard. We'll explain the technique for reading data from the keyboard in a later chapter. For now we'll point out a few highlights, enough that you'll understand how this procedure works.

Example 5.3 Creating a Procedure That Receives Information from the Keyboard

```
<SCRIPT LANGUAGE="VBS">
<!--
Sub CalculateTotalComp()
    Dim intSalary, intBonus, intTotalComp
    intSalary = CInt(InputBox("Enter salary: ", 1))
    intBonus = CInt(InputBox("Enter bonus: ", 1))
    intTotalComp = intSalary + intBonus
    MsgBox "Total Compensation is " & intTotalComp
End Sub
-->
</SCRIPT>
```

Text contained within the quotation marks is displayed on the screen to prompt the visitor to enter information at the keyboard. The integer 1 tells the VB Script engine to display the Cancel button on the screen. You can display one of an assortment of buttons. This is discussed in Chapter 9.

Another trick—the assignment operator (=) is used in this statement. Remember, the assignment operator copies the value of the operand from the right of the operator to the operand on the left of the operator. To the right of the operator is the InputBox(). Actually, it is the value returned by the InputBox() function, which is information entered on the keyboard. And to the left of the operator is a variable. Yes, this statement assigns data entered at the keyboard to a variable.

Now the functionality of the procedure has greatly increased. When called by a VB Script, the procedure prompts the visitor to enter information, and the VB Script engine assigns this information to a variable. This process is repeated once more to collect the bonus value before the procedure has the VB Script engine calculate the total compensation, which is displayed on the screen.

HEY, PROCEDURE, I NEED SOME HELP

Did you see something strange in the VB Script examples that contain the procedure? If you look carefully, you'll realize that these procedures are never executed in the VB Script. Remember, a procedure is a group of statements invoked by the VB Script calling the procedure. If the VB Script does not call for help, the procedure can't help out.

In these examples, we've only created the procedure, we did not call the procedure. A procedure can be called by using the name of the procedure as a statement, known as a *call* in a VB Script. This technique is illustrated in Example 5.4, where the VB Script calls the CalculateTotalComp procedure.

Example 5.4 Calling a Procedure

```
<SCRIPT LANGUAGE="VBS">
<!--
Sub CalculateTotalComp()
    Dim intSalary, intBonus, intTotalComp
    intSalary = CInt(InputBox("Enter salary: ", 1))
    intBonus = CInt(InputBox("Enter bonus: ", 1))
    intTotalComp = intSalary + intBonus
    MsgBox "Total Compensation is " & intTotalComp
End Sub
CalculateTotalComp
-->
</SCRIPT>
```

There is a finer point to note in this example. The procedure is declared before it is called by the script. This is necessary because the VB Script engine must know about the procedure before being told to execute it. The VB Script engine reads the VB Script sequentially, so if the statement that calls the procedure is read first, the VB Script engine could be confused. However, if the order within the VB Script is reversed, the confusion will be avoided.

A VB Script can pass information to a procedure when the procedure is called by placing the information within the parentheses of the name of the procedure. Well, it's a little more complicated than this. Before a procedure can accept information from the VB Script, we must prepare the procedure to receive such data.

The first step is to place the name of the variable that will hold this data between the parentheses of the procedure declaration. This information can then be used within the procedure by referencing the name of the variable. These variables are called *arguments*.

This technique is illustrated in Example 5.5. The name of the procedure contains two arguments within the parentheses: Sub CalculateTotalComp (intNewSalary, intNewBonus). These variables represent salary and bonus data, which are passed to the procedure when the procedure is called from within the VB Script.

Example 5.5 Calling a Procedure and Passing Information to It

```
<SCRIPT LANGUAGE="VBS">
<!--
Sub CalculateTotalComp(intNewSalary, intNewBonus)
    Dim intTotalComp
    intTotalComp = intNewSalary + intNewBonus
    MsgBox "Total Compensation is " & intTotalComp
End Sub
Dim intSalary, intBonus
        intSalary = CInt(InputBox("Enter salary: ", 1))
    intBonus = CInt(InputBox("Enter bonus: ", 1))
    CalculateTotalComp intSalary, intBonus
-->
</SCRIPT>
```

Note that the names of the arguments are different than the names of the variables used when the procedure is called. When the procedure is called, the variables used are intSalary and intBonus. However, the procedure knows this data as intNewSalary and intNewBonus.

Let's see why this is true. Variables intSalary and intBonus are symbols that represent the addresses in memory that contain the salary and bonus information entered at the keyboard. In contrast, variables intNewSalary and intNewBonus are different memory addresses known only to the procedure. These are called *local* or *private variables* if passed by value, and will be discussed later in this chapter.

A few rules must be obeyed when using arguments with a procedure. These are shown in Table 5.1

Table 5.1 Rules for Using Arguments with a Procedure

The position of an argument must correspond to the data passed to the procedure. That is, the first data passed to the procedure is assigned to the first argument, the second data passed to the procedure is assigned to the second argument, and so forth.
Multiple arguments can be used within the parentheses of the procedure declaration as long as arguments are separated by a comma.
The name of an argument must follow the rules used to name a variable. The name of an argument is used in place of the corresponding data within the procedure.
Values passed to a procedure can be literal values, variables, or the results of an expression unless the value is passed by reference.

INSIDE A PROCEDURE

Now that you have the broad strokes of what is required to define and call procedures, let's cover the finer points about using procedures in your VB Script. Procedures are *public* to your VB Script and to other procedures that are available to your VB Script. This means that any procedure can be called from anywhere in the script.

However, certain data are private to a procedure. These are the variables defined from within the procedure. Those variables are not available to statements that are outside of the procedure. These variables also include the variables that are used as arguments to the procedure.

This is an important factor to consider when you define variables for a VB Script. Remember, variable names must be unique to the scope of the variable. Therefore, you cannot have two variables with the name intSalary in the VB Script. However, the scope of variables defined within a procedure begins and ends with that procedure. So you can have a variable defined in your VB Script as intSalary and you can use the same name to define a variable within a procedure. Each variable is an alias for a different address in memory, because the two have different scopes. The scope of the variable defined in the VB Script is the entire script, except the procedure, while the scope of the variable in the procedure is just that procedure.

Another important factor to consider when defining variables within a procedure is that the values assigned to these variables are lost when the procedure ends. So each time the procedure is called, statements within it must redefine the variables and reassign a value to those variables.

There are a few facts that you should know about variables that are used within a procedure before we explore other facets of a procedure. There are two kinds of variables: those variables that are defined using the Dim keyword and those variables that are implied. The implied variables are declared by assigning a value to a variable name without formally using the Dim keyword.

Although a procedure can be called by another procedure, you cannot declare a procedure within another procedure. Each procedure must be declared individually and its functions can be combined with others by calling other procedures as necessary to complete the task. A word of caution: A procedure can call itself. The techno jargon is called *recursion.*

Private vs. Public

Private? Public? Too confusing? Do you wish that computers were made easy to program? A sure way to avoid conflict when defining variables within your VB Script engine is by using one of two magic words, *private* or *public* in your statement that defines a variable.

When you precede the name of a variable with the keyword *private,* the VB Script engine respects your wishes regardless of where you define a local variable in the VB Script. That is to say, a variable will not be available to other parts of the VB Script such as procedures.

Likewise, variables preceded with the keyword *public* are treated by the VB Script engine as global and are available to all parts of the VB Script. This is true even if the variable is defined in a procedure, such as Dim Public intSalary, Private intNewBonus.

This is rarely required by a procedure; however, when it is employed, you must be careful that you don't exceed the available memory reserved for the procedure. Some more techo jargon: this is called a *stack overflow* and could keep your VB Script from executing.

Statements within a procedure continue to be evaluated by the VB Script engine in sequence. This process ends when the last statement is evaluated; then control is returned back to the VB Script or procedure that called the procedure.

However, control can be returned before the last statement in the procedure is evaluated. The magic word to do this is Exit. Place the keyword Exit anywhere in the procedure and the VB Script engine will stop evaluating the procedure. In fact, the Exit keyword can be placed in many statements within the procedure.

This is a good option to keep in your bag of magic tricks. You'll find this especially useful when statements in the procedure must react to specific conditions and not to others. Once the specific condition is encountered, the process will be completed; then there is no need for the procedure to continue with the other statements. This, called *flow control*, will be discussed in detail in the next chapter.

One final point about procedures. A procedure cannot be used in a expression. It is a common practice in VB Script programming to declare a procedure to perform a calculation used repeatedly throughout the VB Script. The statements that perform the calculation are in only one place in the VB Script, which makes it easy to upgrade.

However, we are used to having the procedure return the results of the calculation to the statement in the VB Script that called the procedure. This would allow us to make the calling statement part of a complex expression, as we've seen in previous chapters. But this cannot be done using a procedure, since a procedure does not return a value. Each example in this section performed a calculation and displayed the results on the screen. None returned the results to the calling statement. This is because procedures cannot do this—but function procedures can. That's an upcoming section of this chapter.

HERE'S THE ANSWER

The obvious drawback of using a procedure is that information travels in only one direction, from the VB Script to the procedure. The procedure cannot return a value back to the VB Script unless it changes the value of a public variable.

However, a more traditional approach is to return a value to a VB Script by creating a function procedure. A function procedure is nearly identical to a procedure with some minor, but important, differences. A *function procedure* is declared using the keywords Function and End Function the same way that Sub and End Sub are used to declare a procedure. A function procedure requires a unique name that ends with parentheses. Within these parentheses is information passed to the function procedure from the VB Script. This information is called an *argument*. The same rules that apply to arguments to a procedure also apply to function procedures.

Statements to be evaluated by the VB Script engine when the function procedure is called are contained within the Function...End Function keywords. Like statements in a procedure, statements in a function procedure are evaluated in sequence except when flow control statements are used to redirect the evaluation of statements with a procedure and function procedure.

The name of the function procedure has a dual purpose. First, the name is used to identify the function procedure to the VB Script engine. The name is also used as the name of the variable whose value is returned to the calling VB Script. All return values are of the variant data type.

Example 5.6 shows how a function procedure is declared. Note that the function procedure is declared before it is called by the VB Script. The VB Script must know that the function procedure exists before it can use it.

Example 5.6 Declaring a Function Procedure

```
<SCRIPT LANGUAGE="VBS">
<!--
Dim intSalary, intBonus
intSalary = CInt(InputBox("Enter salary: ", 1))
intBonus = CInt(InputBox("Enter bonus: ", 1))

Function CalcTotalComp(intSalary, intBonus)
    CalcTotalComp = intSalary + intBonus
End Function
Sub CalculateTotalComp(intSalary, intBonus )
```

ByVal, ByRef—Some More Techno Jargon

All the arguments passed to a procedure or function procedure are passed by a technique called *passed by value*. Here we go again, more technical talk. Recall that when a variable is defined, an address in memory is reserved for information. The name of the variable is an alias for the memory address.

When the name of a variable is used within the parentheses of a procedure or function procedure, we are telling the VB Script engine to copy the value of the variable to an argument variable defined within the declaration of the procedure or function procedure. This concept is called *passing by value*. The procedure or function procedure receives the value associated with the variable.

As you probably guessed, there is another way to send information to a procedure or function procedure. This method is called *passing by reference*. Instead of the value of the variable being copied to the argument variable, the address of the variable is passed to the procedure or function procedure.

When information is passed by reference, the VB Script engine does not make another copy of the information in memory. In essence, the VB Script engine uses a corresponding variable on the argument list as another alias for the same address in memory. This saves memory and can also increase the efficiency of the VB Script engine's evaluation of the statement.

Although passing by value is the default choice of the VB Script engine, you can specify the technique you'd like to use by specifying either the ByVal or ByRef keyword to precede the name of the procedure or function procedure such as Function CalcTotalComp(ByVal intSalary, ByRef intBonus).

```
    MsgBox "Total Compensation is " & CalcTotalComp(intSalary, intBonus)
End Sub

CalculateTotalComp()
-->
</SCRIPT>
```

The actual call to the function procedure is made within a compound statement: MsgBox "Total Compensation is " & CalcTotalComp(intSalary, intBonus). This statement calls the CalcTotalComp() function procedure and displays the returning value from the function procedure as part of a string of text.

A look at the CalcTotalComp() function procedure doesn't show anything you haven't seen before during the discussions about procedures, except that the results of the calculation are assigned to the CalcTotalComp variable. This is the variable that holds the value returned to the VB Script that called the function procedure.

The assignment of the return value in the VB Script is implied by constructing a compound statement. A *compound statement* is a VB Script statement that tells the VB Script engine to perform more than one task. In this case, call the CalcTotalComp() function procedure, then concatenate the returning value to a string and display the string in a message box on the screen. The same technique is used to place a call to a function procedure within an expression, which was illustrated in the previous chapter.

Although calling a function procedure as part of an expression or compound statement simplifies the number of statements used in a VB Script, it can also lead to confusion for anyone, except the VB Script engine, who reads the VB Script. It may not be obvious that a call to a function procedure is being made within the statement.

Calling All Procedures!

You can call a procedure or function procedure by simply using the name within a statement of a VB Script. A more formal technique involves prefacing the name of the procedure or function procedure with the Call keyword; for example, intTotalComp = Call CalcTotalComp(intSalary, intBonus).

The use of the Call keyword is optional, since excluding this keyword has the same effect with the VB Script engine whether or not the Call keyword is used appropriately in the statement.

A slightly different approach is shown in Example 5.7. Here, the call to the function procedure is made from within an assignment expression. The value being assigned a variable using the assignment operator is the return value of the function procedure.

Example 5.7 Assigning a Return Value from a Function Procedure to a Variable

```
<SCRIPT LANGUAGE="VBS">
<!--
Dim intSalary, intBonus
intSalary = CInt(InputBox("Enter salary: ", 1))
intBonus = CInt(InputBox("Enter bonus: ", 1))
Function CalcTotalComp(intSalary, intBonus)
    CalcTotalComp = intSalary + intBonus
End Function
Sub CalculateTotalComp(intSalary, intBonus )
    Dim intTotalComp
    intTotalComp = CalcTotalComp(intSalary, intBonus)
    MsgBox "Total Compensation is " & intTotalComp
End Sub
CalculateTotalComp()
-->
</SCRIPT>
```

Chapter 6

Controlling the Flow of Your Web Page with VB Script

Bring on the Traffic Cops

There's no stopping a browser once the browser begins reading your Web page and your VB Script. The HTML file with the embedded VB Script crosses the electronic superhighway and into a visitor's computer, where the browser takes control.

As you would suspect, the browser begins reading your Web page file from the top, then follows by reading every line until the page ends. The browser then sits and waits for further instructions from the visitor.

Although you tell the browser how to display the text contained on your Web page and when to load graphic files and other pages from your Web site, you have no direct control over the behavior of the browser. The browser—actually, the programmers who built the browser—is in charge and can ignore your instructions. In techno jargon this means that the browser does not conform to the same industry standards as used in your Web page.

Now that we showed how powerless you are, let's explore some magic that gives you some control over how your Web page behaves on a visitor's computer. The trick is to use your VB Script to control the flow of your Web page. *Flow control* is more techno jargon for the sequence in which the portions of your Web page are read by the browser.

A common method of retaining limited control of the flow is to use the proper markup tags to allow the visitor to jump to various portions of your Web page. Jumps can be made to either another page of your Web site, another Web site, or to another portion of the current Web page file. These techniques were described in Chapter 2.

While these methods are very useful to a visitor, the jump itself must be made by the visitor. You can offer this option by using the proper HTML markup tag but you can't force the visitor to make the jump. Therefore, many Web site owners design the structure of their Web site pages around visitor-activated jumps.

You are not, however, restrained by this limitation when you embed a VB Script into your Web site page. But, you may be thinking, the VB Script is read sequentially like the Web page itself—and you're correct. The VB Script engine, like the browser, begins reading the VB Script at the top of the script, then evaluates each line until the end is reached. However, you can change how the VB Script engine reads your VB Script by using some of the magic tricks learned in previous chapters and some that we show in this chapter.

Why alter the natural order of your VB Script? This is a good question. In the previous chapters, we used examples that calculated total compensation by adding together the salary amount with the amount of the bonus. Some of those examples told the VB Script engine to perform the calculation only if certain conditions existed, such as if the employee works for a specific department of the company or earns a particular salary. These directions were given to the VB Script engine in the form of an expression.

An expression is used in a control structure that effectively divides the VB Script into two sections. One section contains statements that are evaluated each time the VB Script is read by the VB Script engine. The other section, identified by a control statement, contains statements that are evaluated only if a specific condition exists.

A control statement in the total compensation example enables the VB Script engine to perform the calculations only under the proper conditions. Without the use of a control statement, the calculations might have to be performed every time the VB Script is read. In this chapter, we'll to add an assortment of control statements to your bag of magic tricks.

THE DECISION PLEASE

One of the most useful control statments is the If Then statement. This statement acts as your traffic cop to redirect the sequential reading of your VB Script if the conditions are not safe for the VB Script engine to continue down the path. This is a traffic cop you control—and the VB Script engine always obeys.

The condition is stated in the form of an expression. You know how to formulate an expression. Now you are going to learn how to put your knowledge about the VB Script language to work for you.

The If Then statement defines a block of statements to be evaluated by the VB Script engine only if the expression is true. Otherwise, these statements are ignored by the VB Script engine and the next statement that follows the If Then statement is evaluated.

The VB Script engine recognizes several varieties of the If Then control statement. Probably the easiest to use is the single-statement If Then control statement. This is illustrated in Example 6.1.

Example 6.1 A Simple If Then Statement

```
<SCRIPT LANGUAGE="VBS">
<!--
Dim strDeptNum, intSalary
strDeptNum = "24"
intSalary=20000If
strDeptNum="24" Then intSalary = intSalary * 1.1
-->
</SCRIPT>
```

Notice that a single-line If Then statement is used to instruct the VB Script engine to increase the salary by 10% only if the employee works for Department 24. The conditional expression uses the equal operator to compare the value assigned to the strDeptNum to the literal string of characters 24.

The expression is evaluated to a true or false value by the VB Script engine. If the result is true, then the VB Script engine continues and evaluates the expression that follows the Then keyword. If the result is false, then the VB Script engine moves to the next line in the script.

What line? There is no other line that can be evaluated in the script. The VB Script engine has reached the end of the VB Script and returns control to the browser, which will continue with the next line in your Web page. The same action is taken if the VB Script engine evaluates the statement following the Then keyword.

A word of caution: The simple If Then statement can have a single statement following the Then keyword. If you require more than one statement to be evaluated, then you must turn to another variation of the If Then statement that uses the keywords End If to tell the VB Script engine where the If Then statement block ends.

The If Then statement block is shown in Example 6.2. Notice that the same conditional expression is used; however, the statement that executes when the condition is true is moved to the next line. We can add additional statements above or below this statement without confusing the VB Script engine. When the VB Script engine reads the End If keywords, it knows that the statements within the conditional statements have ended.

Example 6.2 The If Then Statement Block

```
<SCRIPT LANGUAGE="VBS">
<!--
Dim strDeptNum, intSalary
strDeptNum = "24"
intSalary=20000
If strDeptNum="24" Then
    intSalary = intSalary * 1.1
End If
-->
</SCRIPT>
```

SO YOU THINK THIS IS SIMPLE!

Now that you've learned how to use the basic variety of the If Then statement, let's explore more complex ways that you can use it in your VB Script. The If Then statement tells the VB Script engine that, if a condition exists, then do this. But what happens if the condition does not exist? Statements are skipped!

However, in many situations you want a different set of statements to be executed. You need to instruct the VB Script engine that, if a condition exists, then do this; otherwise, do that. This means that one set of statements or the other set is to be executed but not both!

There are a few methods of interpreting this instruction into the VB Script language. For example, you can use another If Then statement and reverse the logic of the conditional expression. This technique is shown in Example 6.3. First, the VB Script engine is told to increase the salary by 10% if the employee works in Department 24. The next If Then statement block reverses this logic. The salary is increased by 20% if the employee does not work in Department 24.

Example 6.3 Multiple If Then Statement Blocks

```
<SCRIPT LANGUAGE="VBS">
<!--

Dim strDeptNum, intSalary
strDeptNum = "24"
intSalary=20000

If strDeptNum="24" Then
    intSalary = intSalary * 1.1
End If

If strDeptNum<>"24" Then
    intSalary = intSalary * 1.2
End If
-->
</SCRIPT>
```

By using two sets of If Then statements, we managed to have the VB Script engine handle any value that can be assigned to the intSalary variable. The value can be either 24 or something else. However, there is a better way to state this in the VB Script language.

Another variation of the If Then statement uses the keyword Else to define statements that are to be evaluated if the conditional statement is false. This is shown in Example 6.4, which is identical to Example 6.3, except the first End If keywords are replaced by the Else keyword. Although both examples are functionally the same, the VB Script engine treats the first example as having two If Then statement blocks and the second example as having only one.

Example 6.4 The If Then Else Statement Block

```
<SCRIPT LANGUAGE="VBS">
<!--

Dim strDeptNum, intSalary
strDeptNum = "24"
intSalary=20000

If strDeptNum="24" Then
    intSalary = intSalary * 1.1
Else
    intSalary = intSalary * 1.2
End If

-->
</SCRIPT>
```

Another technique for using the If Then statement block is to combine multiple blocks into a single block. In some more techno jargon, this is called *nesting* If Then statement blocks. Example 6.5 illustrates this technique. Note that two expressions must be true before the salary increase is given by the VB Script engine.

Example 6.5 Nesting the If Then Else Statement Block

```
<SCRIPT LANGUAGE="VBS">
<!--

Dim strDeptNum, intSalary
strDeptNum = "24"
intSalary=20000

If strDeptNum="24" Then

    If intSalary < 20000 Then
        intSalary = intSalary * 1.1

    End If

End If
-->
</SCRIPT>
```

The first If Then statement block is evaluated. This is called the *outer* If Then statement. If the condition is true, then the next statement within the block is evaluated. This statement happens to be another If Then statement that contains another condition that must be evaluated. This is called the *inner* If Then statement. If this condition is true, then the salary is increased; otherwise, there is no raise in pay.

A word of caution: A common mistake made whenever If Then statements are nested is that the End If keywords are excluded for at least one of the statements. This will cause an error in your VB Script, which could happen while the visitor is reading your Web page.

There are two methods for catching this mistake. First, proofread your VB Script to make sure that you have given the VB Script engine proper instructions. And make sure that you test every VB Script on your own PC before asking visitors to stop by.

Here's a little quiz. Is there an alternative to nesting If Then statements? Sure there is. You can restructure the conditional expression to combine both criteria. This is discussed in Chapter 4. Example 6.6 shows the restructured expression used in Example 6.5. Here the logical operator AND is used to instruct the VB Script engine to compare the results of two conditional expressions. Example 6.5 and Example 6.6 produce the same results.

Example 6.6 Using a Complex Expression to Reduce the Need for Nesting If Then Statements

```
<SCRIPT LANGUAGE="VBS">
<!--

Dim strDeptNum, intSalary
strDeptNum = "24"
intSalary=20000

If strDeptNum="24" AND intSalary < 20000 Then
    intSalary = intSalary * 1.1
End If
-->
</SCRIPT>
```

What happens when more than one condition is possible, and a different set of statements is to be evaluated for each condition? Say that you want to have a different salary increase for each department. The If Then Else statement won't help you give this instruction to the VB Script engine. This statement is used to respond to one of two conditions and not one of many conditions.

However, the If Then Else statement provides a foundation for the final twist of the If Then statement. This variation is the If Then Else If statement, which tells the VB Script engine that if the first expression is true, then do this; otherwise, evaluate the next expression. The second expression has two outcomes, true or false, and depending on the results, one of two sets of statements is evaluated by the VB Script engine.

Confused? Let's use an example to clear the confusion. Example 6.7 provides instructions for three conditions. The first condition is if the department number is 24. The Else If keywords then force the VB Script engine to determine if the department number is 30, if the department number is not

24. Finally, if the department number is neither 24 nor 30, then the keyword Else directs the VB Script engine to evaluate the proper statement.

Example 6.7 The If Then Else If Statement Block

```
<SCRIPT LANGUAGE="VBS">
<!--

Dim strDeptNum, intSalary
strDeptNum = "24"
intSalary=20000

If strDeptNum="24" Then
    intSalary = intSalary * 1.1
Else If strDeptNum="30" Then

    intSalary = intSalary * 1.2

Else

    intSalary = intSalary * 1.3
End If

-->
</SCRIPT>
```

You can include several Else If keywords in an If Then statement. I limited this to one variation because of limited space. However, if you require many alternate conditions, then a Select Case statement is a better technique. This is illustrated in the next section.

JUST A CASE OF CODE

The true magic of a VB Script is that the script can make decisions for you. You've seen that this really isn't much of a magic trick, but what magic trick is once you have learned how it is performed? By using a series of If Then statements you can instruct the VB Script engine how decisions are to be made.

However, this can become tedious, especially when many conditions must be addressed. You have to keep reevaluating the same or similar conditions over and over. A better way to handle this is by using the Select Case statement.

The Select Case statement causes the VB Script engine to evaluate an expression then compare the result to many values, each of which is presented in several Case clauses. Below each Case clause are statements to be evaluated if there is a match.

This technique is illustrated in Example 6.8. The Select Case statement instructs the VB Script engine to compare the value of the strDeptNum variable with each value listed in the Case clause (24 and 30). A match will occur in the first instances since the strDeptNum value is 24. Therefore, the salary will be increased by 10%.

Example 6.8 A Simple Select Case Statement

```
<SCRIPT LANGUAGE="VBS">
<!--

Dim strDeptNum, intSalary
strDeptNum = "24"
intSalary=20000

Select Case strDeptNum

Case "24"
    intSalary = intSalary * 1.1

Case "30"
    intSalary = intSalary * 1.2

End Case

-->
</SCRIPT>
```

Although only a single statement is found beneath each Case clause, you can have any number of statements. The VB Script engine continues to evaluate each statement sequentially until the next Case clause is reached, after which the evaluation process continues with the statement that follows the End Case keywords. In this example, there is no other statement and the script ends. In the Select Case clause, we used a single variable as the test criterion. You can also use any valid expression.

What would happen if you required a series of statements to be evaluated if, and only if, none of the values in the Case clause is matched? The If Then statement can handle it, but can the Select Case statement do the job? Sure, you can use the Case Else clause followed by the statements that are to be evaluated if the criterion doesn't match any value. This is shown in Example 6.9, where the salary is increased by 30%.

Example 6.9 A Select Case Statement with a Case Else Clause

```
<SCRIPT LANGUAGE="VBS">
<!--

Dim strDeptNum, intSalary
strDeptNum = "24"
intSalary=20000

Select Case strDeptNum

Case "24"
    intSalary = intSalary * 1.1

Case "30"
    intSalary = intSalary * 1.2

Case Else
    intSalary = intSalary * 1.3

End Case

-->
</SCRIPT>
```

CAN YOU REPEAT THAT?

The VB Script engine reads your script from top to bottom. You've learned that you can have the VB Script engine take a short side trip by using the

Don't Get Lost, Use REM

Whether you use a series of nested If Then statements or the Select Case statement, your instructions to the VB Script engine can be hard to read—for humans. The VB Script engine has no problem understanding your directions.

You can make it easy to read for yourself, and all of us who like to borrow your VB Script ideas, by indenting statements associated with a particular condition. This is a major component of structured programming.

Then to place the finishing touches on your VB Script, include comments that describe what each condition presents. A comment can be any text but must begin with either an apostrophe (') or the REM keyword. *REM* is short for "remark." In the previous example, we could have placed the comment "REM Increase salary by 30% if no match is found" above the Case Else clause.

Everything on a line that begins with REM or an apostrophe is ignored by the VB Script engine.

If Then statement or a Select Case statement. However, these statements cause the VB Script engine to change direction only temporarily. As soon as the decision is made, the VB Script engine quickly returns to course, headed for the end of the script.

This seems like a logical approach, but there is a serious drawback to sequential evaluation of your script. You may find you need to repeat statements. Take a look at Example 6.10. The VB Script directs the VB Script engine to prompt the user to enter a salary and department number. Once this information is collected, the Select Case statement is used to determine which salary increase is to be calculated, which is displayed in a message box on the screen.

Example 6.10 A Need to Repeat Statements

```
<SCRIPT LANGUAGE="VBS">
<!--

Dim intSalary, strDeptNum
intSalary = CInt(InputBox("Enter salary: ", 1))
strDeptNum = InputBox("Enter department number: ", 1)

Select Case strDeptNum

Case "24"
    intSalary = intSalary * 1.1

Case "30"
    intSalary = intSalary * 1.2

End Case

MsgBox "Your new salary is " & intSalary

-->
</SCRIPT>
```

So far there is no problem, but look closely. How many employees can have their raises calculated? One. What if there are many employees? You could ask the visitor to your Web site to rerun your VB Script. You could replicate statements already in your script for as many times as their are employees. This makes no sense. The best resolution of this problem is to use another kind of control statement to change the way the VB Script engine reads your script. This is called a loop.

A *loop* is a control statement that contains one or more statements to be read continually by the VB Script engine until a specific condition exists. Statements contained within the loop control statements are read sequentially, like statements within the If Then statement. When the last statement is read by the VB Script engine, the VB Script engine returns to the top of the loop and continues to reads statements sequentially.

This can continue until the visitor decides to leave your Web site, which is not being the ideal host. Therefore, you must include an expression the results of which instruct the VB Script engine to exit the loop. As you've seen with the If Then statement, the expression used to test if a condition exists must evaluate to true or false.

Several types of loop control statements are available in the VB Script language. Each one performs basically the same task with slight, but critical, different features. Let's begin with the Do While control loop.

The Do While control loop instructs the VB Script engine to continue to evaluate statements within the Do While block of statements only if the conditional expression evaluates to true. Once the expression turns false, the VB Script engine skips the statements in the Do While block and continues with the statement that follows the keyword Loop. The keyword Loop signifies the end of the Do While block.

Example 6.11 shows how to use a Do While statement in your VB Script. Note that the conditional expression appears to the right of the Do While keywords. The expression tells the VB Script engine to determine if the value of the intSalary is more than zero. This is called a *NULL value,* which is symbolized with two double quotation marks placed side by side. There is no space between the quotation marks.

Example 6.11 The Do While Statement

```
<SCRIPT LANGUAGE="VBS">
<!--
Dim intSalary, strDeptNum
intSalary = 1

Do While intSalary > 0

    intSalary = CInt(InputBox("Enter salary or 0 to quit: ", 1))

    If intSalary > 0 Then
        strDeptNum = InputBox("Enter department number: ", 1)

        Select Case strDeptNum

        Case "24"
            intSalary = intSalary * 1.1

        Case "30"
            intSalary = intSalary * 1.2
```

```
        End Case

        MsgBox "Your new salary is " & intSalary

    End If

Loop

-->
</SCRIPT>
```

After the intSalary and strDeptNum variables are defined, the VB Script assigns these variables an initial value, which is 1. Therefore, the result of the conditional expression in the Do While loop is true.

Since the expression is true, the VB Script engine starts to evaluate expressions within the Do While statement block. You've seen this before, with one exception. After the visitor has finished entering the information, the VB Script engine determines if zero was entered as salary data.

The If Then conditional statement prevents the calculation from occurring if no department number is entered. The Do While loop ends with the keyword Loop, which causes the VB Script engine to return to the top of the loop and reevaluate the conditional expression. If the visitor entered zero for salary, the VB Script engine concludes the loop and moves to the next statement below the keyword Loop, which is the end of the script.

The previous example is simple to understand. The VB Script engine was told to continue to do something while the conditional expression is true. Once the expression is false, the VB Script engine moves on. Although this statement is useful in many situations, another variation of the same Do While statement can help you in unique situations.

We can instruct the VB Script engine to repeat a block of statements until a conditional expression is true. In essence, we're telling the VB Script engine to evaluate the statements within the loop block while the expression is false, then stop when the expression is true.

The magic word that causes this to happen is Until. Instead of using the Do While keywords, we use the Do Until keywords at the beginning of the loop. This is shown in Example 6.12. You'll notice that this is nearly identical to Example 6.11, except for two changes. First, the While keyword is replaced by the Until keyword. Next, the not equal operator (<>) is replaced by the equal operator.

Why? Because we want the VB Script engine to continue to evaluate the statements within the block until the value of intSalary is equal to zero. In the previous example, we wanted to continue to loop while the intSalary did not equal zero. Therefore, as a general rule, if you change a Do While loop to a Do Until loop, you must change the While keyword and reverse the logic of the conditional expression.

Example 6.12 The Do Until Statement

```
<SCRIPT LANGUAGE="VBS">
<!--

Dim intSalary, strDeptNum
intSalary = 1

Do Until intSalary = 0

    intSalary = CInt(InputBox("Enter salary or 0 to quit: ", 1))
    If intSalary > 0 Then

    strDeptNum = InputBox("Enter department number: ", 1)
        Select Case strDeptNum

        Case "24"
            intSalary = intSalary * 1.1

        Case "30"
            intSalary = intSalary * 1.2

        End Case

        MsgBox "Your new salary is " & intSalary

    End If

Loop

-->
</SCRIPT>
```

Both the Do While loop and the Do Until loop have a trait that may not be desirable in all situations. Each of these loops prevents statements within the loop from being evaluated unless the conditional expression results in an appropriate value.

However, you'll find times when you want the statements to be evaluated at least once before the VB Script engine evaluates the conditional expression. Previous examples illustrate this point.

In these examples, we instructed the VB Script engine to determine if the salary entered by a visitor contains a zero value. However, we asked the VB Script engine to answer this question before we asked the user to enter the salary. We performed a little magic of our own by initializing the intSalary variable with 1 so that the VB Script engine read the statements within the loop.

Now let's have the VB Script engine evaluate the statements within the loop at least once before deciding whether or not to continue with the loop. We accomplish this by moving the While and Until keywords to the bottom of the loop. This is shown in Examples 6.13 and 6.14. In both cases, the VB Script engine receives the response from the visitor before the evaluation is made, which takes place at the end of the loop.

Example 6.13 The Do Loop While Statement

```
<SCRIPT LANGUAGE="VBS">
<!--

Dim intSalary, strDeptNum
Do
    intSalary = CInt(InputBox("Enter salary or 0 to quit: ", 1))

    If intSalary > 0 Then

    strDeptNum = InputBox("Enter department number: ", 1)
        Select Case strDeptNum

        Case "24"
            intSalary = intSalary * 1.1
```

```
        Case "30"
            intSalary = intSalary * 1.2

        End Case

        MsgBox "Your new salary is " & intSalary

    End If

Loop While intSalary > 0

-->
</SCRIPT>
```

Example 6.14 The Do Loop Until Statement

```
<SCRIPT LANGUAGE="VBS">
<!--

Dim intSalary, strDeptNum
Do

    intSalary = Cint(InputBox("Enter salary or 0 to quit: ", 1))

    If intSalary > 0 Then
        strDeptNum = InputBox("Enter department number: ", 1)
        Select Case strDeptNum

        Case "24"
            intSalary = intSalary * 1.1

        Case "30"
            intSalary = intSalary * 1.2

        End Case

        MsgBox "Your new salary is " & intSalary

    End If

Loop Until intSalary = 0

-->
</SCRIPT>
```

Before we leave the topic of Do loops, another kind of loop is available in VB Script but is not recommended. This is the While Wend loop. Microsoft does not recommend using this loop because this has the same function as the Do While loop. For completeness, we've included a sample of the While Wend loop in Example 6.15.

Example 6.15 The While Statement

```
<SCRIPT LANGUAGE="VBS">
<!--

Dim intSalary, strDeptNum
intSalary = 1
While intSalary = 1

    intSalary = CInt(InputBox("Enter salary or 0 to quit: ", 1))

    If intSalary > 0 Then
        strDeptNum = InputBox("Enter department number: ", 1)
        Select Case strDeptNum

        Case "24"
            intSalary = intSalary * 1.1

        Case "30"
            intSalary = intSalary * 1.2

        End Case

        MsgBox "Your new salary is " & intSalary

    End If

Wend

-->
</SCRIPT>
```

LET'S TAKE THIS ONE AT A TIME

The loops explored so far in this chapter cause the VB Script engine to continually execute statements within the loop block as long as the conditional expression is true or until the conditional expression exists. This depends on which loop is used in the VB Script.

Another bit of magic specifies the number of times that the statements within the loop block are to be evaluated. This is made possible by using the For Next loop. In essence, the For Next loop tells the VB Script engine to loop through the loop block a specific number of times.

In contrast to the loops already presented in this chapter, the For Next loop has no conditional expression. Example 6.16 shows how the For Next loop is used in a VB Script. The For Next loop requires that a variable be defined that is assigned incremental values during each revolution of the loop. In this example, the intCounter is used for this purpose. Although we chose to name the variable intCounter, any valid variable name will do.

Example 6.16 The For Next Statement

```
<SCRIPT LANGUAGE="VBS">
<--

Dim intSalary, strDeptNum, intCounter

For intCounter = 1 To 4
    intSalary = CInt(InputBox("Enter salary or 0 to quit: ", 1))

    If intSalary > 0 Then
        strDeptNum = InputBox("Enter department number: ", 1)
        Select Case strDeptNum

        Case "24"
            intSalary = intSalary * 1.1

        Case "30"
            intSalary = intSalary * 1.2

        End Case

        MsgBox "Your new salary is " & intSalary

    End If
Next

-->
</SCRIPT>
```

Get Me Out of Here!

Incorporating a loop into your script can be very useful and reduce s the amount of coding to complete your script. However, sometimes you need to leave the loop immediately, without the VB Script engine finishing evaluating the remaining statements in the loop.

You can exit the loop at any time by using one of the forms of the Exit statement. In a previous chapter you saw the Exit statement used to leave a procedure or a function procedure. The same basic concept applies to loops. Once the Exit statement is evaluated by the VB Script engine, the VB Script engine stops readings statements in the loop block and exits the loop immediately.

There are three forms of Exit statements. The Exit Do statement is used to exit a Do loop. The Exit For statement is used to leave a For loop, which will be discussed later in this chapter. Finally, Exit by itself is used to leave a procedure.

In each case, the VB Script engine begins reading the statement that follows the end of the loop. If the loop is nested (one loop within another loop), then control moves from the inner (nested) loop and returns to the outer loop.

Next, a sequential range of values must be specified. This tells the VB Script engine the number of times the statements within the loop are to be evaluated. In Example 6.16, the VB Script engine is told to begin with the value 1 and stop after value 4. The keyword To is used to separate the starting and ending values of the range.

These can be any numeric value or expression. Therefore, we can modify this VB Script by changing the starting value from 1 to 2. This will cause the VB Script engine to loop three times through the loop block rather than four times, which is the case in Example 6.16.

The actual values of the range are irrelevant to the execution of the For Next loop except as incremental counters. There is an exception. You can create a VB Script that uses the intCounter variable. Say you want to create an arithmetic times table like those you remember from grammar school. If you want the five times table with a range of 1 through 12, then all you need to do is define the For Next range as being from 1 through 12. Each value in the range is assigned to the intCounter variable, then the intCounter variable can be used in the expression that multiplies the intCounter variable by 5. The five times table will be automatically produced when the loop ends.

The For Next loop sequentially steps through the specified range. This means that the visitor in the previous example will be asked four times to enter a salary and department number. Each time, the VB Script will calculate the salary increase. This is called a *single-step process*.

However, you can have the VB Script engine skip a specific number of incremental steps by using the Step keyword in the For Next Step loop statement. This is shown in Example 6.17. Here the VB Script engine is instructed to move through the range, skipping every other value.

Example 6.17 The For Next Step Statement

```
<SCRIPT LANGUAGE="VBS">
<!--
Dim intSalary, strDeptNum, intCounter

For strCounter = 1 To 4 Step 2
    intSalary = CInt(InputBox("Enter salary or 0 to quit: ", 1))

    If intSalary > 0 Then
        strDeptNum = InputBox("Enter department number: ", 1)
        Select Case strDeptNum
        Case "24"
            intSalary = intSalary * 1.1

        Case "30"
            intSalary = intSalary * 1.2
        End Case

        MsgBox "Your new salary is " & intSalary

    End If

Next

-->
</SCRIPT>
```

Animation, Please

The For Next loop is a key component of displaying information in an animated way when you have no formal animation software. Let's see how this trick is performed. Animation is the display of an image on the screen. Each time it is shown, the image is moved slightly. By quickly displaying the images, the visitor gets the feeling that the image is really moving on the screen.

There are more formal techniques for performing animation on your Web site, some of which I'll discuss later in this book. However, you can explore animation by using the For Next loop. An image can be placed on the screen by specifying the coordinates of the upper left corner of the image as it relates to the screen.

For example, 0,0 is the upper left coordinate of the screen. The first zero represents the number of positions (pixels) going down the screen and the second zero represents positions going across the screen (left to right).

So, if you want to move an image across the screen, you can specify the full range of positions as the horizontal range of the positions on the screen. Say there are 1000 horizontal positions on the screen. The range would be from 0 to 999: For intCounter = 0 To 999.

Next, position the image on the screen specifying the vertical position as a literal value and the horizontal position as the intCounter variable. Each revolution of the For Next loop will cause the image to be displayed at a different horizontal position on the screen.

Two other pieces of magic are necessary to complete this illusion. First, after each revolution of the loop, the image must be erased; otherwise, you'll end up with the new images partially overlying the previous images, similar to a fanned deck of cards. An image is erased by displaying the image using the background color.

The second piece of magic is to use the Step keyword to control the speed at which the image moves across the screen. For example, For intCounter = 0 To 999 Step 2 moves the image twice as fast as the original For Next statement since the VB Script engine skips every other horizontal position on the screen.

You can reverse direction by changing the range and using a minus value as the step like this: For intCounter = 999 To 0 Step -2.

In this example, statements in the loop block will be evaluated by the VB Script engine twice, although the range specifies four times. On the first pass, the value 1 is assigned to the intCounter variable. On the second pass, the VB Script engine is told to skip the value 2 and assign the value 3 to the intCounter variable. This is the effect of using the Step 2 keyword in the script. Likewise, the VB Script engine will skip the value 4 and try to assign the value 5 to the intCounter variable. Because this is beyond the range of values, the loop ends.

Like the other loops discussed in this chapter, the For Next loop can be nested. This means that for every value in the range of the outer For Next loop, an inner For Next loop is evaluated.

WHAT'S NEXT?

Now that you have a good understanding of how to define data—procedures, finction procedures, having the VB Script engine make decisions for you, and controlling the flow of your script—we'll turn our attention back to managing information.

In the next chapter, you'll learn about arrays and how to group together related data to streamline the way the VB Script engine manipulates data.

Chapter 7

VB Script and Arrays

LET'S GROUP IT TOGETHER

We began our look at the VB Script language by examining information manipulated by statements in the VB Script. Information—data—is stored in memory as a literal value or assigned to a variable.You'll recall that a literal value is a number or a character contained within double quotation marks. On the other hand, a variable is an alias for an address in memory where some value is stored. The value is assigned to the variable from within a VB Script. A literal differs from a variable in that the literal value does not change during the life of the VB Script. However, a variable can be assigned several values—each time a new value replaces the current value of the variable.

No, we are not going to rehash everything you've learned about variables. We're just reviewing some of the basics so you can learn how to group variables under the same name. The variables discussed so far in this book can be assigned only one value and are technically called *scalar variables*.

Each scalar variable requires a unique name. On the surface this does not seem to pose much of a problem. However, imagine if you have to create many variables, each one containing a different employee number. For each employee, you must devise a unique variable name.

If you are successful in naming all these variables, your next problem is to reference these variables within your VB Script. This is no problem if a handful of variables are used; however, the task becomes unwieldly when you must deal efficiently with 25 or more variables within the VB Script.

There must be a better way. The VB Script language provides a way to group like data under a common name called an array variable. Unlike the scalar variable, an *array variable* can have many values. Each value is assigned to an element of the array variable. And those elements are identified by numbers, not names.

This means that you can declare an array called EmpNum that has 30 elements and each element can be assigned an employee number.

I DECLARE YOU AN ARRAY

An array is created by using the Dim keyword. The variable name is followed by the number of elements in the array enclosed within parentheses, as shown here: Dim Array(30). This statement creates an array that has 30 elements.

The name of the array variable should reflect the contents of the data stored in the array. All the rules for naming a variable described in detail in Chapter 3 apply to naming an array variable as well. An array variable also follows the same scope rules as a variable. For example, an array variable defined in a procedure is local to the procedure and cannot be accessed by any other part of the VB Script. Any array variable defined in the main segment of the script is public and can be accessed by other parts of the VB Script.

Data is stored to an element of an array variable by using the assignment operator. This is illustrated in Example 7.1. Note that this statement is very similar to that used to assign a value to a variable. However, there is one difference. The name of the array variable must specify the number of the element that is to be assigned the data. The number of the element is called an *index number*.

Example 7.1 Declaring an Array Variable

```
<SCRIPT LANGUAGE="VBS">
<!--
Dim EmpNum(30)
EmpNum(0) = "2401"
EmpNum(1) = "2402"
-->
</SCRIPT>
```

A word of caution: while working with an array variable, you can easily fall into a trap that many new VB Script programmers discover the hard way. We'll point this out now before you get caught. Index numbers used to identify elements of an array variable are zero based. That's some more techno jargon for saying that the first element of the array variable is number 0, not number 1!

In Example 7.1, you'll see that the first assignment statement instructs the VB Script engine to store the literal string 2401 at the memory address referenced by array variable element EmpNum(0). Likewise, the second element of the array variable, EmpNum(1), is assigned the string 2402.

Many new VB Script programmers confuse the index number used to declare an array variable with the index number used to reference an element of the array variable. When declaring an array variable, the index number is one based. That is, if you want 30 elements, then the index number is 30 when declaring the array variable, not 29.

However, when accessing the elements of the array variable, the index number is zero based. Therefore, if you want to access element 30, you would use index number 29. Still confused? A little practice will reinforce these differences in your mind.

Once data is assigned to an array variable element, the element can be used throughout your VB Script in the same manner as you would use a variable. Example 7.2 illustrates this point by displaying in a message box the value assigned to the first element of the array variable.

Example 7.2 Using a Value Assigned to an Array Variable

```
<SCRIPT LANGUAGE="VBS">
<!--
Dim EmpNum(30), strNum
EmpNum(0) = "2401"
MsgBox "Employ: " & EmpNum(0),1
EmpNum(1) = "2402"
strNum = EmpNum(1)
MsgBox "Employee: " & strNum,1
-->
</SCRIPT>
```

In the same example, the value assigned to the second element of the array variable is assigned to another variable, the contents of which later will be displayed in a message box on the screen. In both cases, the name of the array variable is used along with a reference to the corresponding index number of the element that contains the data.

You can see how an array variable is used to group like data. But why use an array variable? The answer is illustrated in Example 7.3. In the previous section, you learned that a major drawback of using scalar variables—single-value variables—is that it is cumbersome to manipulate large amounts of data stored in those variables. Remember, each variable has a unique name.

However, the array variable can perform some magic of its own that makes working with large amounts of data a breeze. Notice in Example 7.3 that a For Next loop is used to manipulate information in the array variable. The first statement in the For Next loop uses a single statement to initialize values of four elements of the array variable.

Example 7.3 Using an Array Variable in a Loop to Assign Values and Calculate Values

```
<SCRIPT LANGUAGE="VBS">
<!--
```

```
Dim Salary(4), intTotal, intCounter
intTotal = 0
For intCounter = 0 To 3
    Salary(intCounter) = 20000
    intTotal = intTotal  + Salary(intCounter)
Next

MsgBox "Total Salary: " & intTotal,1
-->
</SCRIPT>
```

The trick is in the index number. The value range of the For Next loop contains the same values as the index numbers used to identify specific elements of the array variable. Therefore, we use the intCounter variable as the index number for the array variable elements in the assignment statement.

Likewise, the second statement in the For Next loop uses the same technique for stepping through each element of the array variable. However, this statement is adding the salary value assigned to each element to the intTotal variable, the contents of which later will be displayed in a message box on the screen.

Ready for a quiz? Try rewriting Example 7.3 without using an array variable. How many statements would you need to perform the same task? Which method is more efficient?

MAYBE I NEED 20...NO, MAKE THAT 25...ON THE OTHER HAND, I'LL TAKE 30

Now you know the trick of working with large amounts of data. Well, you really know only part of the trick—there's more. An obvious limitation of using an array variable is that you must know the number of elements you will require when you declare the array varaible.

Of course, this is obvious. However, you may not know how many you will need. Perhaps you've written a VB Script that collects information from the visitor, then stores the information in an array variable. You've seen this kind of VB Script in the previous chapter, where a loop was used to repeatedly evaluate the data input statement.

As you may recall, the loop terminated when the visitor entered zero. Until then, data was continually being read from the keyboard. So there was no way for the programmer to know in advance how many array variable elements would have to be stored in memory.

Could this be a show stopper? One solution is to create an array variable the size of which exceeds the reasonable number of entries that can be expected from a visitor. The actual size of the array variable is a guess, but a wrong guess limits the amount of data that can be gathered from the visitor or wastes memory.

There is a better way. You can create a dynamic array variable. A *dynamic array* variable enables you to have the VB Script engine change the number of elements in the array variable while the VB Script is being evaluated. This technique is shown in Example 7.4.

Example 7.4 Changing the Size of an Array Variable

```
<SCRIPT LANGUAGE="VBS">
<!--
Dim EmpNum
Redim EmpNum(2)
EmpNum(0) = "2401"
EmpNum(1) = "2402"
Redim Preserve EmpNum(3)
EmpNum(2) = "2403"
-->
</SCRIPT>
```

In this case, a dynamic array variable is declared by using the Dim statement, then assigning the results to the name of the array variable. Note that no index value is placed between the parentheses. This tells the VB Script engine that the size of the array variable will be redimensioned later in the VB Script.

The Redim keyword is used to change the number of elements in the array variable. The Redim keyword instructs the VB Script engine to look for the EmpNum array variable, then change the dimension of the array variable to have two elements.

The real advantage to using a dynamic array variable is that the size of the array variable can be changed anywhere in the VB Script. Example 7.4 shows this technique. After the EmpNum dynamic variable is declared, the size is changed to two elements. The VB Script instructs the VB Script engine to assign values to each of the array variable elements.

This is the same technique used to solve the data entry problem we spoke of earlier in this section. If the VB Script is to collect additional information from a visitor, the VB Script engine must be told to increase the size of the array variable by one element.

To avoid making a common mistake, whenever the size of the array variable is changed, the index number used to define the new size must include all of the index numbers used to identify existing elements. In the previous example, the size changed from two elements to three elements. The Redim statement used the index number 3 to resize the array variable.

Caution: Normally, when a dynamic array variable is resized, all the information assigned to the array variable is lost. However, you can instruct the VB Script engine to retain the information as the array variable is resized by using the Preserve keyword. Example 7.4 illustrates the proper use of the Preserve keyword.

LET'S GO TO THE NEXT DIMENSION

Did you ever wonder how to create a table of information in your VB Script? Can you keep a secret? It's done by using an array variable. Actually, a multidimensional array variable. Yes, more techno jargon.

Multidimensional is a term right out of the Twilight Zone. So let's bring us back to earth and take a closer look at this concept of dimensions. Have you ever worked with a spreadsheet? If you have, you've been working in two dimensions. The first dimension is a row and the second dimension is a column.

So far in this chapter, we've been talking about a single-dimension array variable. This is like talking about a row, where each row is an element of the array variable. Columns are the second dimension, which we haven't talked about, until now. VB Script can handle a maximum of 60 dimensions, but we'll concentrate on two-dimensional array variables.

Example 7.5 shows how to declare a two-dimensional array variable. Here, the variable is called Emp and the Dim statement assigns 30 rows (first dimension) and two columns (second dimension). We can add other dimensions by specifying another value in the declaring statement.

Example 7.5 Declaring a Multidimensional Array Variable

```
<SCRIPT LANGUAGE="VBS">
<!--
Dim Emp(30,2)
Emp(0,0) = "2401"
Emp(0,1) = 20000
Emp(1,0) = "2402"
Emp(1,1) = 20000
-->
</SCRIPT>
```

Take a closer look at this array variable. For each of the 30 rows there are two columns. This forms a matrix that looks very similar to a spreadsheet or a table of a database. Each element in the first dimension (rows) represents a single employee. In this case, we can have a maximum of 30 employees. The second dimension (columns) is used to store information about the employee.

The first element (column) of the second dimension is assigned the employee's employee number, and the second element is assigned the employee's salary. A particular element can be referenced by specifying the coordinates of the elements. A coordinate is the index number of the corresponding first and second dimensions (row and column) of the array variable element. In this example, Emp(1,1) specifies the coordinates for the second row and the second column of that row.

Values in a coordinate are accessed practically the same way you access an element of a single array variable. Just specify the name of the array variable and the index numbers of the coordinate. You can then use the multidimensional array variable element as you would use a single-dimensional array variable element. This is illustrated in Example 7.6.

Example 7.6 Using a Value Assigned to a Multidimensional Array Variable

```
<SCRIPT LANGUAGE="VBS">
<!--
Dim Emp(30,2)
Emp(0,0) = "2401"
Emp(0,1) = 20000
Emp(1,0) = "2402"
Emp(1,1) = 20000
MsgBox "Employ: " & Emp(0,0) & "Salary:" & Emp(0,1)
MsgBox "Employ: " & Emp(1,0) & "Salary:" & Emp(1,1)
-->
</SCRIPT>
```

Now let's put the concept of a multidimensional array variable to work. You want to tally the salary of all the employees. No problem. All we need to do is loop through the multidimensional array variable and add together the salaries. Example 7.7 shows how this is done.

Example 7.7 Using a Multidimensional Array Variable in a Loop to Assign Values and Calculate Values

```
<SCRIPT LANGUAGE="VBS">
<!--
Dim Emp(30,2), intCounter, intTotal
intTotal = 0
Emp(0,0) = "2401"
Emp(1,0) = "2402"
Emp(2,0) = "2403"

For intCounter = 0 to 2
    Emp(intCounter, 1) = 20000
    MsgBox "Employ: " & Emp(intCounter,0) & "Salary:" & Emp(intCounter,1)
    intTotal = intTotal  + Emp(intCounter,1)
Next

MsgBox "Total Salary: " & intTotal ,1
-->
</SCRIPT>
```

Ready for another quiz? You can use a similar technique for finding information in the array variable. Simply loop through the array variable and compare the employee number with the employee number for which you are searching. The If Then statement comes in handy for this chore. Once a match is found, break out of the loop and display the message "Found" in a message box. Why don't you try writing this VB Script. You know how to do it.

GETTING FANCY

The VB Script language contains a host of tricks that modify the way the VB Script engine handles an array variable. We'll look at these new tricks so that you can add them to your toolbag. Let's begin with the Public and Private keywords. These were mentioned earlier in this book, when we explored the use of variables within procedures. However, a quick review is in order since they also affect how the VB Script engine works with an array variable.

Although an array variable is declared and assigned information, this information may not be available to every part of your VB Script, because some array variables are isolated from the rest of your script. How do you know if the array variable can be used throughout your VB Script? The answer depends on where the VB Script is declared and whether or not the Public or Private keyword is used as part of the declaration. As you recall from our previous discussion about procedures, a variable and an array variable that are declared within the procedure can be used only by statements within the procedure. Other procedures and the main segment of the VB Script cannot use the variable or array variable declared in a procedure.

In contrast, a variable or array variable declared in the main segment of a VB Script, outside a procedure, can be used throughout the script, including by procedures. The techno jargon for specifying parts of the script that can use a variable or an array variable is the term *scope*.

The scope of an array variable can be modified by using either the Public or Private keyword when the array variable is declared. The Public keyword makes the array variable available to the entire script; the Private keyword is used to limit the scope of the variable to a segment of the VB

What Is That Value?

An advantage of using the VB Script language is that variables are all of the same type, called a *variant*. The VB Script engine handles the memory requirements for a variable based on the type of information assigned to that variable. For example, if an integer is assigned to a variable, the VB Script engine will treat the variable as an integer subtype.

As you learned in Chapter 3, variables of like subtypes can be used together in expressions. However, this procedure has a disadvantage in that there is no indication other than an assignment statement as to the subtype of a variable.

Now for some magic. The keyword VarType( ) lets the VB Script engine tell you the subtype of a variable. The VarType() function requires that you place the name of the variable within the parentheses. VarType() returns a numeric value that indicates the subtype of the variable. Table 7.1 decodes this return value for you.

Table 7.1 Return Values and Definitions for the VarType() Function

Value	*Variable Type Description*
0	Empty (uninitialized)
1	Null (no valid data)
2	Integer
3	Long integer
4	Single-precision floating-point number
5	Double-precision floating-point number
6	Currency
7	Date
8	String
9	OLE automation object
10	Error
11	Boolean
12	Variant (used only with arrays of variants)
13	Non-OLE automation object
17	Byte
8192	Array

Script or a procedure. These keywords are used with an array variable in the same way as with the scalar variables shown in Chapter 5.

Make information disappear right before your eyes. A little dramatic, but you can make the data you assigned to an array variable disappear from memory with the function Erase(). Erase() causes the VB Script engine to perform differently depending on whether the array variable is declared as a dynamic array variable or a fixed array variable. In the case of a dynamic array variable, the size of the array variable is set to 0 and the memory used by the array variable is released. The Redim keyword must be used to set the size of the array variable before it can be used again in the VB Script.

In contrast, Erase() resets the values that are assigned to elements of a fixed array variable. Numeric elements are set to 0 and string elements are set to 0 length. However, memory used by the fixed array variable is not released. Therefore, you redefine a fixed array variable after it has been erased. Example 7.8 illustrates how to erase an array variable.

Example 7.8 Erasing an Array Variable

```
<SCRIPT LANGUAGE="VBS">
<!--
Dim EmpNum
EmpNum = Array()
Redim EmpNum(2)
EmpNum(0) = "2401"
EmpNum(1) = "2402"
Erase(EmpNum)
Redim EmpNum(3)
EmpNum(2) = "2403"
-->
</SCRIPT>
```

What size is the array variable? The answer seems obvious but it may not be easy to answer in a complex VB Script that changes the size of a dynamic array variable frequently in the script. To answer this question, simply use the magic word UBound().

UBound() requires that you specify the name of the array variable and the number of the dimension you want the VB Script engine to size for you. The dimension number is optional. If the dimension is not included in the statement, then the VB Script engine assumes that you want to know the upper boundary of the first dimension. UBound() returns an integer that represents the maximum number of elements in the specified dimension of the array variable. You can see how to do this in Example 7.9.

Example 7.9 Using UBound( )

```
<SCRIPT LANGUAGE="VBS">
<!--
Dim EmpNum
Redim EmpNum(2)
EmpNum(0) = "2401"
EmpNum(1) = "2402"
Redim Preserve EmpNum(3)
EmpNum(2) = "2403"

MsgBox "Upper: " & UBound(EmpNum, 1)

-->
</SCRIPT>
```

COMING UP

You've heard a lot of talk about strings. You know how to declare a variable as a string subtype and how to assign values to a string variable. However, you can do much more with strings in your VB Script.

Coming up in the next chapter is a complete discussion of strings. You'll learn how to assemble a long string of information from several smaller strings. You'll learn how to break down a long string into several smaller strings, and how to locate data within a long string.

You can't afford to miss this next chapter, since much of what a VB Script does is to manipulate string information. Stay tuned for the tricks of strings.

Chapter 8

Strings Attached to Your Web Page

I Got Some Strings

The most important data you'll be using with your VB Script are strings. Actually, a string is a subtype of the variant data type you learned about in Chapter 3. Just think of a string as a series of characters that are attached to each other; when they appear together on the screen or in a report, these characters become meaningful to the visitor to your Web site.

Characters used in a string can be any characters that appear on the keyboard. These include the letters of the alphabet, numbers, and symbols such as the asterisk. All are considered characters that can be part of a string.

These characters are associated with each other by enclosing the characters within double quotation marks. You've seen this done throughout the previous chapters in this book. So, if you want the letters B-o-b to be related as a string, you must placed them in an appropriate literal, like this, "Bob".

In this example, "Bob" is a string literal that cannot change during the running of the program since this string is typed into your VB Script. *Hard coded* is the techno jargon for this technique. String literals are commonly used as the text of messages you display to visitors to your Web site. String literals also are captured from the keyboard when users enter information in response to your questions.

Although you can use a string literal as part of a function that displays information on the screen, such as the MsgBox() procedure, you'll find it necessary to assign a string literal to a variable or an element of an array variable. This technique is shown in Example 8.1.

Example 8.1 Strings and Numerics

```
<SCRIPT LANGUAGE="VBS">
<!--
Dim strString, intNumber
strString = "1234"
intNumber = 1234
-->
</SCRIPT>
```

Two variables are defined in the first statement of this VB Script. Although the prefixes str and int are used, the prefix has no bearing on the subtype of the variable. You'll recall this from our discussion about variables in Chapter 3. The prefix is just a symbol that tells the programmer the subtype of the variable. No one but you enforces this rule. The VB Script engine doesn't recognize the prefix as anything but part of the name of the variable.

However, what does matter is the kind of data assigned to the variable. In the second statement, a string literal is assigned to the strString variable. This statement informs the VB Script engine that the variable's subtype is a string. Likewise, in the third statement, the assignment of the integer value to the intNumber variable makes the intNumber variable an integer subtype.

Why is this important? The answer becomes obvious when you try to add the variables strString and intNumber. Both variables seem to contain the same value of 1234. However, the VB Script engine treats them as radically different when these values are stored in memory.

Each character is represented in memory by the ASCII value of the character in the form of a byte. Therefore, the string version of the value 1234 requires four bytes, with each byte being interpreted by the VB Script engine as the ASCII value of the character.

In contrast, the value 1234 that is assigned as an integer to the intNumber variable is a number, not a character. On some computers, the number 1234 is stored in memory as two bytes. So when the VB Script engine looks at the value stored in memory, it knows to interpret the bytes as a numeric value.

So, what does this mean to you? Well, you can't add the characters 1234 to the number 1234. But don't be too concerned. As you probably guessed, you can make this problem go away. We'll examine how to convert a string value to a numeric value and a numeric value to a string value later in this chapter.

PUT THEM TOGETHER

Consider a string a list of characters. You probably have many of these lists within your VB Script, that is, many strings. And, like numbers, sometimes you need to combine strings to form a larger string. Also like numbers, the VB Script language provides two operators that can join strings. Sound too stringy for you? You'll be combining strings frequently when you set out to build a fancy Web site that will attract visitors. In addition, this trick is not at all difficult to perform.

The trick of combining strings is called *concatenation*. In the VB Script techno jargon, you are said to be concatenating two strings to form a new string that contains the smaller strings. The operators that instruct the VB Script engine to perform this magic are the addition operator (+) and the ampersand operator (&).

Microsoft recommends that you use the ampersand operator instead of the addition operator when concatenating strings. Although both operators give the VB Script engine the proper instruction, the ampersand operator helps to avoid confusion when you and other VB Script programmers read your script. The ampersand operator is used only to combine strings, whereas the addition operator is also used to sum two numeric operands.

So you're still not sure that you'll ever need to concatenate two strings? Well, a look at Example 8.2 might change your mind. Two string variables are assigned the first and last name of a person, respectively. The task is to display each full name on the screen in a message box.

Example 8.2 Concatenating Strings

```
<SCRIPT LANGUAGE="VBS">
<!--
Dim strFirstName, strLastName
strFirstName = "Jim"
strLastName = "Smith"
MsgBox strFirstName & strLastName ,1
MsgBox strFirstName & " " & strLastName,1
-->
</SCRIPT>
```

You could use two message boxes, one to display each string variable; however, that wouldn't seem correct on the screen. The only way to resolve this problem is to combine the string variables as they are displayed in the message box, which is shown in the fourth statement in this example.

If you have the VB Script engine evaluate this VB Script you'll notice something peculiar. The last name immediately follows the first name. This isn't correct—there should be a space between the names; however, we didn't give the VB Script engine the instruction to place a space between the names. Remember, the VB Script engine is not smart enough to read your mind. It just does exactly what it is told to do. If you don't give it the instructions, the VB Script engine doesn't do it.

In this case, we must include a space between the strings. A space? You may not normally think of a space as being a character. Nor do you think of a tab being a character, either. This is because we don't see a space or a tab. These are called *white space characters*.

Before we can concatenate the space character to the first-name string variable, we must convert the character into a literal string. We do this by placing double quotation marks around the space character. This makes the space a string. Next, we use another ampersand operator to complete the concatenation, as shown in the fifth statement in Example 8.2.

GET RID OF THOSE SPACES

A space within a string is used to help us identify words of a string when the characters are displayed on the screen or in a report. However, sometimes spaces will creep into a string in places where they just don't belong. You'll find this happening when information is gathered from a visitor. Inadvertently, a visitor might press the space bar in the wrong place. Remember, the space is a character that is read by the VB Script engine and assigned to a string variable like any other character read from the keyboard.

A good VB Script programmer, however, will assume that the information submitted by the visitor is not clean and has one or more space characters at the beginning or at the end of the string. You can have the VB Script engine remove those unwanted spaces by saying a few magic words: RTrim(), LTrim(), and Trim().

Example 8.3 illustrates how these words are used in your VB Script to remove unwanted spaces. We created three literal strings that contained the first, middle, and last names of a person. Notice that the first name begins with a space and the middle name has spaces before and after the name. The last name ends with several spaces. The VB Script engine's job is to remove those spaces.

Example 8.3 Removing Unwanted Spaces in a String

```
<SCRIPT LANGUAGE="VBS">
<!--
Dim strFirstName, strMiddleName, strLastName
strFirstName = "  Jim"
str strMiddleName = "  Bob   "
strLastName = "Smith   "
```

```
strFirstName = LTrim(strFirstName)
strMiddleName = Trim(strMiddleName)
strLastName = RTrim(strLastName)
MsgBox (strFirstName & " " & ,1)
-->
</SCRIPT>
```

The spaces must be removed before the strings are concatenated; otherwise, it will be difficult to remove the spaces contained within the concatenated string. Note that we said "difficult"—it is still possible by using other magic that you'll learn a little later in this chapter.

For now, let's make it easy on ourselves and remove the spaces before the names are joined together. First, we'll use the LTrim() function to remove spaces at the beginning of the string. This is shown in the fifth statement in the example. The LTrim() function returns all the characters of the string minus the leading spaces.

Did you notice something unusual with this statement? The return value of the LTrim() is assigned to the same variable that contains the spaces. This is perfectly acceptable. When the LTrim() function has completed its operation, the contents of the variable are no longer required and therefore can be overwritten by the returning value—the string without the leading spaces. You can use this same technique with any function.

The next step is to remove the spaces from the beginning and the end of the middle name. Here, the Trim() function is called into play. The Trim() function instructs the VB Script engine to remove leading and trailing spaces and return the remaining characters to the VB Script. This occurs in the sixth statement. The returning characters are assigned to the strMiddleName variable.

The last name contains trailing spaces, so we must use the RTrim() function to remove spaces at the end of a string. This function returns characters except those space characters that are found as the last characters of the string. Once the spaces are removed from the variables, the strings, separated by a space, will be joined together so the complete name of the person can be displayed on the screen.

A CAPITAL MISTAKE, BUT WE'LL FIX IT

Can you think of another common mistake a visitor to your Web site might make when entering a name into your VB Script? How about capitalization of a name? Let's say that you want a visitor to sign in to your guest book when arriving at your Web site, then throughout the visit you want to address your visitor by his or her first name.

How do you do this? We'll show you in the next chapter how to receive information from your visitor and assign that data to a string variable. For this exercise, let's assume that the visitor's first name is already assigned to a string variable.

The question is, are the letters in the first name properly capitalized? The visitor could have used a mixture of upper and lowercase letters even though he intended to capitalize the first letter and use lowercase letters for the remaining characters. You would hate to repeat the visitor's mistake, especially when you're trying to make a first impression.

Well, you've probably guessed it. A few magic words take care of this problem for you. These are UCase() and LCase(). All right, they're not words but functions.

Example 8.4 shows how these functions are used to ensure correct capitalization in the string. Note that we created two strings. The first string contains the first character of the name. The remaining characters are in the second string. Is this cheating? A visitor wouldn't enter his or her name as two strings. The visitor's name is received by the VB Script engine as one string and your VB Script must instruct the VB Script engine to separate the string. We'll show you how to do this in the next section.

Example 8.4 Changing the Case of a String

```
<SCRIPT LANGUAGE="VBS">
<!--
Dim strFirstCharacter, strOtherCharacters
strFirstCharacter = "j"
strOtherCharacters = "IM"
strFirstCharacter = UCase(strFirstCharacter)
strOtherCharacters = LCase(strOtherCharacters)
MsgBox strFirstCharacter & strOtherCharacters,1
-->
</SCRIPT>
```

Upper and Lower

An uppercase letter is a different character than a lowercase letter, according to your computer. Each character on the keyboard has a unique number, called the *ASCII value* of the character. This value is stored in the memory of the computer.

This means that the letter *A* has an ASCII value that is different from the letter *a*, although to us, both letters have the same meaning. Likewise, white space characters such as the space and tab characters also have their own ASCII values.

When the VB Script engine reads the value stored in memory, it recognizes the value as a number, not a character. However, the VB Script engine refers to the subtype of the variable that is used as an alias for that address in memory to decide how that number is to be represented in the VB Script.

If the subtype of the variable is a string, then the VB Script engine knows that the value is an ASCII value that must be converted to a particular character on the keyboard.

So, there is an important difference between an uppercase letter and a lowercase letter. This becomes a concern when we display strings on the screen, but it is also a critical factor when strings are compared, as will be seen shortly.

When the UCase() and LCase() functions convert a character to the opposite case, the functions simply change the ASCII value of the character. The VB Script engine then interprets the value and displays the character in the proper case.

To begin, assume these characters were separated by the VB Script engine and assigned to two string variables. The fourth statement in Example 8.4 shows how the UCase() function is used to change all the characters in the string to uppercase. The uppercase characters are returned by the function and assigned to the same string variable. Note that we said all the characters in the string. Since the first character of the original string is already separated, only the first character is changed to uppercase.

The same technique is used in the fifth statement, except the LCase() function is used to change all the characters to lowercase. Once the conversion is complete, the string variables are concatenated to display the first name of the visitor in a message box.

BEHIND THE SCENES OF THE PASSWORD SCRIPT

Another bit of magic that you can perform with strings is to have the VB Script engine compare each character of both strings. Why do this? Have you ever heard of password protecting your Web site? You'll need to compare two strings. Here's how it's done.

Example 8.5 creates two string variables. The first string variable, strPassword, is assigned the string literal that is the password. The second string variable, strInput, is the password entered by a visitor. For this example, we'll assume that the visitor has already entered the password. The next chapter will show you how to read information from the keyboard.

Example 8.5 Comparing Strings

```
<SCRIPT LANGUAGE="VBS">
<!--
Dim strPassword, strInput
strPassword = "Joe sent me"
strInput = "Mike sent me"
If StrComp(strPassword, strInput) = 0 Then
    MsgBox "Welcome!"
Else
    MsgBox "Get out of here!"
End If
-->
</SCRIPT>
```

Next, the StrComp() function instructs the VB Script engine to compare the two strings. This comparison is made by performing arithmetic. Arithmetic? These are letters of the alphabet, not numbers. Not so!

The StrComp() function returns a 0 if there is a match. A –1 is returned if the first string is less than the second string, and a +1 is returned if the second string is less than the first string. If either string has nothing assigned to it, then the StrComp() function returns a NULL—a nothing.

In Example 8.5, the If then statement is used to evaluate the return value of the StrComp() function. If the return value is 0, then a message box welcomes the visitor; otherwise, the visitor is told to get out.

TAKING APART A STRING

Strings contain information that can be modified by your VB Script engine, as you've seen throughout this chapter. The success of this manipulation depends on how well you master the trick of picking apart portions of the string while the visitor is looking at your Web site. As with most of the tricks we've shown you in this book, segmenting a string isn't difficult. All you need is a little practice, and a few standard functions, of course.

First we must determine the length of the string. This information will be required to properly tell the VB Script engine where to begin chopping away at the string. The magic word that tells the VB Script engine the length of a string is Len(), as shown in Example 8.6.

Example 8.6 Manipulating Parts of a String

```
<SCRIPT LANGUAGE="VBS">
<!--
Dim strFullName, strFirstName, strMiddleName, strLastName
strFullName = "Jim Bob Smith"
MsgBox "Length is: " & Len(strFullName)
strFirstName = Left(strFullName, 3)
str strMiddleName = Mid(strFullName,5,3)
strLastName = Right(strFullName, 5)
MsgBox strFirstName & " " & strMiddleName & " " & strLastName
-->
</SCRIPT>
```

In this example, we assign a string literal that contains a person's full name to the strFullName string variable. The Len() function is then called to instruct the VB Script engine to determine the number of characters in the string. The length is an integer value that is then returned by the Len() function and displayed on the screen in a message box. The return value can also be assigned to an integer variable and used in another function to copy a portion of the string.

Let's continue with the example. As well as learning the length of the string, the task of this VB Script is to extract the first, middle, and last names of the person from the strFullName string variable. The fifth statement in the VB Script tackles the first step; that is, copying the first name to the strFirstName variable.

The Left() function is used to instruct the VB Script engine to begin this process by going to the leftmost character of the strFullName string variable and copying three characters beginning with that position. This means the Left() function returns the string "Jim". Note that the Left() function requires two arguments. The first argument is the string. This can be in the form of a string variable, a literal string, or a string that is returned from another function or procedure. The second argument specifies the number of characters to be copied, beginning with the leftmost character of the string in the first argument.

Now we turn our attention to the person's middle name. Since the characters that we want appear somewhere in the middle of the string, we can't use the Left() function. Instead, we use the Mid() function. This function requires three arguments. The first argument is the string, which can be in the same form as described for the Left() function. The second argument is the starting position within the string. This is the number of the character from the leftmost character where the VB Script engine will being copying characters. The last argument is the number of characters to be copied.

In this example, the VB Script engine is told to go to the fifth character in the strFullName string variable and copy the next three characters. The return value of the Mid() function is the string "Bob".

The final step in this process is to use the Right() function to retrieve the last name of the person. The Right() function instructs the VB Script engine to move to the last character in the string and then begin copying. This function requires two arguments. The first argument is the string and the second argument is the number of characters that are to be copied, beginning with the last character in the string.

Search and a Little Magic

Wait a minute! How do you know that the first name always has three letters and the last name has five letters? You caught us. You don't know. However, you do know all those magic words that let you instruct the VB Script engine to take apart a string into those names.

Look at this in Example 8.7. This VB Script appears to be very confusing and filled with techno jargon, but there is nothing in this VB Script that you haven't seen before in this book. All we did was to combine the previously learned material into a script that separates the first and last name from a string without knowing where the first name ends and the last name begins.

Example 8.7 Using the Len() Function to Copy Parts of a String

```
<SCRIPT LANGUAGE="VBS">
<!--
Dim strFullName, strFirstName, strLastName
Dim intCounter, strCharacter
strFullName = "Jim Smith"
For intCounter = 1 To Len(strFullName)
    strCharacter = Mid(strFullName, intCounter,1)
    If strCharacter = " " Then
        strFirstName = Left(strFullName, intCounter-1)
        strLastName = Right(strFullName, Len(strFullName)-intCounter)
    End If
Next
strLastName = Trim(strLastName)
MsgBox strFirstname & " " & strLastName
-->
</SCRIPT>
```

We'll take this VB Script apart step by step to make this clear. The first two statements in the script declare six variables. The strFullname variable is assigned the string that consists of the first and last name. The strFirstName and strLastName variables will be assigned the first and last name strings.

We've declared two utility variables. *Utility variable* is a general name given to a variable that assigns the values that help the VB Script engine complete a task. The values assigned to these variables later are thrown away and not displayed on the screen.

The first of these utility variables is the intCounter. The intCounter is used to record iterations of the For Next loop. The strCharacter variable is assigned each character of the strFullName variable so the VB Script engine can determine where the first name ends.

Before we review the logic of this VB Script, we must make an assumption: the first name and last name are separated by a space character. Therefore, the VB Script engine needs to locate the space character in the strFullName string. Once the character position of the space is known, the VB Script can separate the strFullName string into the first and last names.

After assigning the full name to the strFullName string variable, the For Next loop is entered and the VB Script engine is instructed to examine each character of the string. Notice that the Mid() function is used for this purpose. The Mid() function returns the character of the strFullName string variable that is located at the position specified by the value of the intCounter.

Confused? Let's take this slowly. The first time around the loop the value of the intCounter is 1. Therefore, the Mid() function is told to go to the first character of the full name "John Smith" and return one character. The J is returned by the function and assigned to the strCharacter variable.

Next, the VB Script engine compares the character "J" with a space character. If there is no match, then the For Next loop increments intCounter, which now has a value of 2. The Mid() function then goes to the second character of the "Jim Smith" string and returns one character, which is *i*. This character is compared to the space character and since they don't match, the loop continues.

The space character is encountered when the intCounter variable has the value of 4, so then the If Then Else clause of the For Next loop is exercised. Use Left() to assign strFirstName to the first (intCounter – 1) characters of the strFullName.

In the second statement, the Right() function returns the characters of the last name, which are assigned to the strLastName variable. Boy, those arguments of the Right() function appear a bunch of complex techno jargon again. Don't fret! You already learned everything that appears as arguments to the Right() function. Let's take this apart piece by piece.

The first argument, strFullName, is the variable that contains the full name of the person. The second argument specifies the number of characters that are to be copied. This number isn't obvious, since we asked the VB Script engine to calculate this value for us. The last argument is actually an expression. This expression uses the Len() function to determine the length of the string, which is 9. Next, the value of the intCounter, 4, is subtracted from the length of the string. The result of this subtraction is 5, which is the number of characters that must be copied to form the person's last name.

As a general practice, strLastName is trimmed of leading and trailing spaces, then both are displayed on the screen in a message box (strFirstName cannot contain any spaces based on the algorithm we used).

Is there an easier way to locate the space in the string? Yes, you can use another trick to have the VB Script engine find the space without using a loop and performing string comparisons. We didn't show you this trick right away because you needed to learn how to manage complex manipulation of strings.

Now that we showed you the hard way, let's use the magic word InStr() to make life a little easier. The InStr() function instructs the VB Script engine to search a string for another string, then return the position of the first character. This is shown in Example 8.8. Although this example searches for a single-character string, you can use any length string as the search criterion for the InStr() function.

Example 8.8 Finding One String within Another String

```
<SCRIPT LANGUAGE="VBS">
<!--
Dim strFullName, strFirstName, strLastName, intLastNamePos
strFullName = "Jim Smith"
intLastNamePos = InStr(strFullName, " ")
If ( intLastNamePos > 0 ) Then
    strFirstName = Left(strFullName, intLastNamePos - 1)
    strLastName = Right(strFullName, Len(strFullName) - intLastNamePos)
    strLastName = Trim(strLastName)
    MsgBox strFirstName & " " & strLastName
Else
    MsgBox "There are no spaces."
End If
-->
</SCRIPT>
```

The InStr() function requires two arguments. The first argument is the string that is going to be searched. You can specify the string as a literal string or a string variable, which is the case in this example. The second argument is the search criterion. In this case, we are searching for the space character in the strFullName string.

You'll notice that the return value of the InStr() function is assigned to the intLastNamePos variable. This variable will contain the position of the space character in the strFullName variable. In our example, the position of the space is character 4.

Although we know that there is a space in the strFullName string, you can't be sure that this is the case in each VB Script you write. Therefore, before the VB Script engine begins to use the position of the search criterion, the VB Script must instruct the VB Script engine to determine if the search string exists.

You can have the VB Script engine make this test by including an If Then statement in the script, as we have done, to compare the results of the InStr() function. The return value of the function should be greater than 0; otherwise, the search criterion will not be found.

Once we're sure that the space is found, we can instruct the VB Script engine to copy the first name from the string. This is performed by the Left() function. The first argument is the strFullName string variable. The second argument is the number of characters that are to be copied, beginning with the first character of the strFullName string. Note that this value is the position of the space minus 1. Remember, we don't want the space copied.

Next, the VB Script engine is told to copy the characters of the last name. The Right() function is used for this purpose. The first argument is the strFullName string variable. The second argument is the number of characters that are to be copied. For this value, we instruct the VB Script engine to perform a little arithmetic. The VB Script engine is told to determine the length of the full name, then subtract the position of the space from it. The length is nine characters. The space is in the fourth character position. The starting position is the fifth character position. The number of characters to be copied is five.

The next statements are used to remove leading and trailing spaces from strLstName before the strings are displayed in a message box.

I Change You to a Number; Now You Are a String

Earlier in this chapter we talked about the problem that could arise working with data of unlike subtypes. You may recall that a literal string of number characters such as "1234" cannot be used in arithmetic. This means that you'll be disappointed in the results when you add "1234" with 1234.

We also learned that a magic word will instantly transform the numeric characters of a string to a numeric subtype. Now's the time to learn the magic word: Val(). Actually, this is a VB Script language function that converts a string to a number value.

This technique is shown in Example 8.9. The Val() function requires one argument, which is the string that will be converted to a number subtype. This function returns the numeric equivalent of the string.

Example 8.9 Converting Strings to Numbers and Numbers to Strings

```
<SCRIPT LANGUAGE="VBS">
<!--
Dim intNumber, strString
intNumber = 42
strString = CStr(intNumber)
intNumber = Val(strString)
-->
</SCRIPT>
```

Well, if you can turn a string into a number, you'd probably guess that you can reverse the process. In fact, you can choose from two words that change a numeric value into a string: Str() and CStr().

Like the Val() function, both the Str() and CStr() functions require one argument. In these cases, the argument is the number. The return value of both functions is the string equivalent of the number.

Which function do you use? Either way, you must consider the subtle difference between the two before making your selection. The Str() function assumes that the number in the argument conforms to the American standard for representing values, that is, a period is used as the decimal symbol and commas separate the whole number digits into sets of three.

In other countries, however, these symbols are reversed, that is, a comma is used to symbolize a decimal and periods are used to separate sets of whole numbers.

Your VB Script must be sensitive to this because anyone from around the world can visit your Web site and provide you with numeric information. The best way to sensitize your VB Script to this possible condition is to use the CStr() function in place of the Str() function. The CStr() function recognizes the international conventions for numbers and properly converts the number to a string.

In Example 8.9, a numeric literal is assigned to the intNumber variable. The value of this variable is then converted to a string using the CStr() function, and the return value is assigned to the strString variable. The last statement of the VB Script uses the Val() function to change the strString value to a number, which is assigned to the intNumber variable.

NEXT TIME

Throughout these chapters, we've talked about receiving information from a visitor and displaying your message on the visitor's computer. Did you ever wonder how this is done? You'll learn this in the next chapter.

Chapter 9

Moving Data In and Out of Your Web Page

THE COFFEE KLATCH

Can we talk—to your visitor, that is? The VB Script engine will let you do almost anything and the VB Script engine will let your VB Script hold a conversation with a visitor to your Web site. The conversation, however, is less chatty and more in the form of questions and answers.

You've already had a taste of conversing with a visitor to your Web site as you learned various VB Script programming techniques in previous chapters. Frequently we used a message box to display the results on the screen. However, we just scratched the surface when it comes to communicating with your Web visitor.

The techno jargon used for this give and take between the VB Script and the Web site visitor is an *interactive Web site*. Aren't all Web sites interactive? No, at least not in the true sense of the term *interactive*.

All Web sites use hypertext files (see Chapter 2) to provide limited interactivity with the Web site visitor. This is made possible by linking keywords and phrases to hypertext jumps to bookmarks within the same page or to other files on the Web site. By double-clicking on the highlighted words, the visitor instructs the browser to display other information.

While some visitors may consider this an interactive Web site, there are serious capabilities that are not available in hypertext. That's where the VB Script comes into play. You already learned various techniques that enable your VB Script to manipulate information received from a visitor. Now we turn our attention to gathering that information from the keyboard of the visitor's computer.

If you are familiar with a graphical user interface (GUI) you know that information can be entered into an application in various ways. Likewise, a number of methods can be employed to display information on the screen. For example, data gathering can be achieved by using radio buttons, check boxes, list boxes, drop-down boxes, or text boxes. Each of these is called an *object* and contains a method for displaying information associated with the object.

Objects are a key element of a VB Script application. We will discuss two simple ways to use a few of these objects to gather and display information in your script. You can begin to perform these magic tricks immediately, then move on to more complex objects later in this book.

I NEED INPUT

The easiest way to gather information from a visitor is to use the InputBox() function. This function causes the VB Script engine to display a dialog box that contains several objects. These objects are a text box, an OK button, and a Cancel button.

Example 9.1 shows how to use the InputBox() function in your VB Script. One argument is used with the InputBox() function—the string that prompts the visitor to enter information in the text box. It is critical that the prompt actually describes the data your VB Script expects to receive from the visitor.

Example 9.1 Gathering Data from the Visitor

```
<SCRIPT LANGUAGE="VBS">
<!--
Dim strVisitorName
strVisitorName = InputBox("Enter your first name and last name: ")
-->
</SCRIPT>
```

In this example, we asked the visitor to enter his or her first and last names. This directive is explicit. If we changed the prompt to ask for the visitor to enter his or her name, there is room for doubt. Do you want my first name or my last name?

Even if we asked the visitor to enter his or her full name, there can be confusion. Do you want first name then last name or the last name then the first name? You must be explicit in your directions because the visitor is in no position to ask for clarification.

Who cares how the name is entered? You do. Your script is going to do something with this information. As seen in the previous chapter, a VB Script can direct the VB Script engine to separate the information into components. The techno jargon for this operation is *parsing* the data. But before the VB Script engine can perform this task, the information must be in a certain format. The prompt tells the visitor the proper format for the data.

Enough about the prompt. Let's move on to the action performed by the VB Script engine. This simple function causes the VB Script engine to display a dialog box on the screen that shows the prompt along the left side of the text box. Beneath the text box are the OK and Cancel buttons. The cursor is automatically positioned inside the text box waiting for the visitor to enter the information.

The visitor enters a name, then selects the OK button to continue with your VB Script. The OK button is the default selection and, therefore, also can be selected by the visitor pressing the Enter key. The VB Script engine reads the Text property of the text box, then assigns this string to the strVisitorName string variable.

HTML vs. InputBox() When Receiving Data

You might be puzzled when we said that you cannot receive information from your Web site visitor unless a VB Script is embedded in your Web page. In fact, you can receive data from the visitor by using the <INPUT> HTML tag, as shown in Chapter 2.

However, this technique is dramatically different than using the InputBox() function within your VB Script. The <INPUT> HTML tag enables your Web page to collect information from the visitor, which is then sent to an e-mail address. This information must be reformatted into an acceptable form so that your application can use the data.

In contrast, information entered into a VB Script using the InputBox() function is already in a format that can be used by the VB Script. In most cases, you'll find the InputBox() function a more appropriate way to gather information from visitors to your Web site.

Text property? Each object contains various properties. The information entered into the text box is called its *text property*. The InputBox() function automatically instructs the VB Script engine to read the text property of this box. As you'll learn later in this book, your VB Script can directly instruct the VB Script engine to read and modify properties of an object.

AND YOUR TITLE IS...

If you execute the VB Script in Example 9.1, you'll notice that the title bar of the dialog box might contain strange-looking text. Where did this come from? It came from the VB Script engine. The bar at the top of the dialog box, called the *title bar*, contains the title of the dialog box.

By default, the VB Script engine uses the name of the application as the title for the dialog box. This is the text that appears on the title bar. Do you want to change this? You can.

You change the text that appears in the title bar by using the title argument of the InputBox() function. Example 9.2 illustrates how this is done. Note that the first argument to the InputBox() is the string that prompts the visitor to enter information into the text box. The second argument is the string that will appear in the title box of the dialog box.

Example 9.2 Setting the Title for the InputBox( ) Function

```
<SCRIPT LANGUAGE="VBS">
<!--

Dim strVisitorName

strVisitorName = InputBox("Enter your first name and last name: ", "Guest
Book")

-->
</SCRIPT>
```

You can give the dialog box any title you wish. In this case, Guest Book seems to be an appropriate title. The title should relate to the activity taking place within the dialog box. There are two kinds of titles that you should avoid.

First, don't use the title to prompt the visitor. A string such as "Enter your name" is not a professional title for a dialog box, although collecting the visitor's name is the objective of the dialog box. Leave such directions for the InputBox() prompt.

Second, don't use a string that is too general as the title for the dialog box. For example, "Data gathering" is too broad a phrase to be used as a title. Keep the title well focused on the purpose of the dialog box, like a headline of a newspaper rather than a sentence.

I'LL GIVE YOU A HINT

Whenever you design a VB Script to collect information from visitors to your Web site, you should make sure that the questionnaire is easy to understand and simple to use. Remember, the visitor has no opportunity to open a dialog with you while entering information into your questionnaire.

I'll forego any lengthy discussion on writing proper questions since this goes beyond the scope of this book. But, the questionnaire should be tested on your friends, then fine-tuned before exposing it to the whole world.

However, making data input easy is right up our alley. Probably the best way to encourage a visitor to fill out a data entry form is to answer the questions yourself. Well, at least, you could provide the most common response so that the visitor need only confirm the answer then move on to the next question.

You can provide a suggested answer by establishing a default value for the question. Actually, you are supplying a default value for the InputBox(). Example 9.3 shows how this is done. In this example, the question "Where do you go on Friday night?" is posed to the visitor in a dialog box. The title of the dialog box is "Personal Survey."

Example 9.3 Setting a Default Value in the InputBox()

```
<SCRIPT LANGUAGE="VBS">
<!--
Dim strFridayNight

strFridayNight = InputBox("Where do you go on Friday night? ", "Personal
Survey","Stay Home")

-->
</SCRIPT>
```

The third argument of the InputBox() function is the default value, which is "Stay Home." The words *Stay Home* appear in the text box when the dialog box is displayed on the screen. If the visitor selects the OK button or presses the Enter key, the default value is automatically returned by the InputBox() and assigned to the strFridayNight string variable.

However, the visitor has the chance to change the default value by overriding the entire text or by editing the text using the standard graphical user interface techniques for text editing.

Although the default value shown in Example 9.3 is a literal string, you can use a string variable in place of the literal string. Let's say that you want a response—or part of a response—to another InputBox() as the default value of another InputBox(). In this case, assign the previous response to a string variable, then use that value as the default value of the second InputBox(). Use part of the response? Sure, you learned how to take apart a string in the previous chapter.

MOVE THE BOX OVER THERE—NO, PUT IT HERE

If you've tried the sample VB Scripts in this chapter, you soon learned that the VB Script engine nearly centered the dialog box in the screen. The dialog box is centered horizontally but is situated one-third of the distance down the screen.

The position of the dialog box is in your control. You don't have to accept the default position of the dialog box on the screen. Instead, you can specify a new position by supplying the InputBox() function with two new arguments: the xpos and ypos arguments.

The xpos argument is the numeric expression that determines the horizontal distance between the left edge of the dialog box and the left edge of the screen. The ypos argument sets the measurement for the vertical distance of the upper edge of the dialog box from the top of the screen.

The values of xpos and ypos are integers that represent the number of twips. (Yes, some more techno jargon that is described in the box entitled "Twip.") Example 9.4 changes the position of the dialog box from the near center position to a position in the upper left corner of the screen.

Example 9.4 Positioning the Dialog Box on the Screen

```
<SCRIPT LANGUAGE="VBS">
<!--
Dim strFridayNight

strFridayNight = InputBox("Where do you go on Friday night? ", "Personal
Survey","Stay Home", 0,0)
-->
</SCRIPT>
```

Twip

No, this isn't a derogatory word for someone who acts differently than you. A *twip* is a unit of measurement that is used to identify positions on the screen. Each inch of your screen contains about 1,440 twips.

Why create another unit of measurement? This is a good question, and here is the good answer. Images on your screen are created by using pieces of pictures called *pixels*. In many programming languages, you can use a function to specify a particular pixel, then change the color of the pixel to make part of the image appear on the screen.

If every visitor to your Web site used the same resolution display screen, specifying positions on the screen in the form of pixels would give you control over where the image is placed. However, nothing is that simple when you deal with computers. Some visitors will have higher resolution displays than others. This means that the image will not appear the same on every screen.

A serious problem presents itself. How can you ensure that your highly graphical Web page using a VB Script is displayed uniformly? Twips, of course. The twip measurement is independent of the resolution of the display screen. That is, twips is a unit of measurement used to proportionally display images, including characters, on the screen regardless of the resolution of the display.

Although integer values are used as the xpos and vpos arguments, you can also use an expression that results in a similar value. Some VB Script programmers devise a complex algorithm (a way to do something) that instructs the VB Script engine to position the dialog box in relation to other objects on the screen. This will prevent the dialog box from overlapping another object.

NEED HELP?

Sometimes it is just not practical to provide a default answer in an InputBox(). For example, if you ask the visitor for his or her name, you can't supply a suggested response. However, this doesn't mean that you can't help a visitor supply data to your Web site.

You can include a full-fledged graphical user interface help document similar to those found in Windows applications. The help document is commonly created by using an authoring tool such as ForHelp, which lets you assemble the document in a way similar to creating an HTML document by using a Web page authoring tool.

Each topic in the help document is assigned a unique number, which is later used to display the topic on the screen. This is like bookmarks in an HTML file. When the bookmark is selected, the browser will jump to the text that corresponds to it.

A complete discussion on how to build a help document is beyond the scope of this book. We recommend that you purchase a help document authoring tool to build a help document for your VB Script application. This tool will enable you to create detailed instructions for filling out your questionnaire, assign numbers to topics within the help document, and save the document in the help file format.

Once you've created the help document, you can offer this assistance to your visitor by providing the name of the help file and the topic you want displayed as arguments to the InputBox() function. This technique is illustrated in Example 9.5.

Example 9.5 Assigning a Help Document to the InputBox()

```
<SCRIPT LANGUAGE="VBS">
<!--
Dim strFridayNight

strFridayNight = InputBox("Where do you go on Friday night? ", "Personal
Survey","Stay Home", 0,0,"persurvy", "23")

-->
</SCRIPT>
```

Note that there are two additional arguments to the InputBox() function. The sixth argument is a literal string, "persurvy", that contains the name of the help document file. The next argument is "23", which is called the *context number* that instructs the VB Script engine to display the text of topic 23. We'll assume that this topic provides further instruction to the visitor on how to answer the question "Where do you go on Friday night?"

Whenever these functions are included as arguments to the InputBox() function, the VB Script engine automatically displays the Help button in the dialog box. When the Help button is selected by a visitor, the VB Script engine causes topic "23" of the "persurvy" help document to be displayed on the screen.

The visitor can scroll through the help document or select hypertext to jump to another part of the document. The visitor will return to the InputBox() dialog box after exiting the help document.

DISPLAY YOUR OWN MESSAGE

In earlier chapters, you've seen how the MsgBox() function is used to display information on the screen. We simply passed the string that we wanted displayed as an argument to the MsgBox() function. Now let's take a few moments to fully explore the other features of this function so you can do much more with the MsgBox() function.

When your VB Script calls the MsgBox() function, the VB Script engine takes your message and displays it in a text box that is contained within a dialog box centered on the screen.

The dialog box can also contain one or more control buttons. You decide which control buttons are displayed in the dialog box by specifying a numeric value as the second argument of the MsgBox() function.

Table 9.1 contains the values that correspond to the control buttons. For example, if you want the OK button displayed in the dialog box, then the second argument of the MsgBox() function is 0. Each value in the table corresponds to a specific selection of control buttons in the dialog box. In examples shown previously in this book, we used the value 1 with the MsgBox() function so that both the OK and Cancel buttons were displayed.

Table 9.1 Control Button Values

Value	*Description*
0	Display OK button only
1	Display OK and Cancel buttons
2	Display Abort, Retry, and Ignore buttons
3	Display Yes, No, and Cancel buttons
4	Display Yes and No buttons
5	Display Retry and Cancel buttons
16	Display Critical Message icon
32	Display Warning Query icon
48	Display Warning Message icon
64	Display Information Message icon

Another attribute of the message box that you can modify is which of the buttons displayed in the message box is the default button. As you may recall, the default button is the one that is highlighted when the message box is displayed on the screen. The visitor can select this button by simply pressing the Enter key.

Table 9.2 contains the values that must be added to the control button values in Table 9.1 to instruct the MsgBox() to display the appropriate control buttons and make one of them the default button. Add these values? Yes, try adding a value from each of these tables and you'll notice that each combination produces a unique sum, making it easy for the VB Script engine to know which combination you selected.

Table 9.2 Values That Set the Default Control Button in the Dialog Box

Value	*Description*
0	First button is default
256	Second button is default
512	Third button is default
768	Fourth button is default

Now let's complicate the equation by including another variation. Do you want the message box to be application modal or system modal? The modal attribute prevents the visitor from doing anything else with the computer until a response is given to your message box. This means that the visitor must press one of the control buttons in the message box dialog box before continuing with your VB Script.

The severity of this restriction is controlled by the modal attribute of the message box. There are two settings for this attribute: application modal and system modal. *Application modal* means that the visitor is prevented from continuing with your application until a response is registered. However, the visitor can still access other applications.

In contrast, the *system modal* setting prevents the visitor from using any application on his or her computer until a control button is selected in the message box. You register your choice between application modal and system modal by adding another value to the second argument to the MsgBox() function. These values are shown in Table 9.3

Which should you choose? The answer depends on the nature of the message in the message box. If the message pertains only to your VB

Table 9.3 Values That Determine the Modality of the Dialog Box

Value	*Description*
0	*Application modal:* The user must respond to the message box before continuing work in the current application
4096	*System modal:* All applications are suspended until the user responds to the message box

Script, then application modal is the proper choice. However, if the message is notifying the visitor of a system-wide issue, then the system modal setting should be selected.

Example 9.6 illustrates how to make these modifications to the message box. You'll notice that the value 0 is used as the second argument to the MsgBox() function. This places the OK button in the message box, sets this button as the default button, and makes the message box application modal.

Example 9.6 Adding Control Buttons to the Message Box

```
<SCRIPT LANGUAGE="VBS">
<!--
MsgBox "Welcome to my Web site.", 0
-->
</SCRIPT>
```

Yes! Wait, No!

The MsgBox() function can perform more magic than simply displaying a message on the screen. This function can also be used to receive information from a visitor. A visitor cannot enter free-form text in the MsgBox(). This is reserved for the InputBox() function. However, the choice of control button made by a visitor can be reported back to your VB Script by the VB Script engine.

This is made possible by assigning the return value of the MsgBox() to a variable or using the MsgBox() as part of an expression. Table 9.4 contains a listing of integer values that are returned by the MsgBox() when a visitor selects a corresponding control button.

Note in Example 9.7 that a message box is displayed that asks the visitor if he or she likes your Web site. Only two control buttons are displayed in the message box: Yes and No. The response is reported by the MsgBox() and assigned to the intReponse variable.

Next, the VB Script evaluates the visitor's response to determine which control button is selected. The If Then statement is then used to present an appropriate reply to the visitor's selection.

Table 9.4 Return Values from the MsgBox() Function

Value	*Button Chosen*
1	OK
2	Cancel
3	Abort
4	Retry
5	Ignore
6	Yes
7	No

Example 9.7 Evaluating the Return Value of the MsgBox() Function

```
<SCRIPT LANGUAGE="VBS">
<!--
Dim intResponse
intResponse = MsgBox "Do you like my Web site?", 4
If intResponse = 6 Then
    MsgBox "I knew you'd like it.", 0
Else
    MsgBox "I'd like to see you do better!", 0)
End If
-->
</SCRIPT>
```

Adding a Title and Help

You can round out the features that enhance the message box by including a title and on-line help. The title is the text that appears on the title bar of the message box dialog box. The text is passed to the MsgBox() as the third argument to the function. This is identical to the technique described earlier in this chapter to create a title for the input box dialog box.

Also like the input box dialog box, you can include on-line help. On-line help enables the visitor to press the Help control button in the dialog box to display content-sensitive help text, which is similar to the hypertext

Creating Multiple Lines

Text displayed in a message box and a prompt in the input box can be expanded to more than a single line by using some ASCII magic. The VB Script engine is told to move to a new line on the screen by inserting two invisible characters into the text: the carriage return and line feed characters.

A *carriage return* character tells the VB Script engine to move to the beginning of the line. The *line feed* character gives the instruction to move to the next line on the screen. The combination of these instructions places the cursor at the beginning of the next line.

As you learned in the previous chapter, each character on the keyboard is represented by a numeric value—the ASCII value. When the VB Script engine "sees" the ASCII value in memory, it knows that you want a particular character on the screen.

Some characters, called *white space characters* (such as the tab character), are invisible to us. Although we can't see them, they still have an ASCII value that is recognizable by the VB Script engine. The carriage return and line feed characters are white space characters with the ASCII values of 13 and 10, respectively.

How can you place these characters into your text? You concatenate them to the text. Here's how it works. Say your message is "Welcome! Take your shoes off and stay a while." You want to place "Welcome!" on the first line.

The first step is to convert the ASCII values of the carriage return and line feed characters to characters. Remember, the ASCII value is an integer. The Chr() function handles the conversion for you. This function requires the ASCII value as the argument to the function and returns the character that corresponds to the ASCII value. This character can then be concatenated to the text that is to appear on the first line. And the text that is to appear on the second line is concatenated to the carriage return and line feed characters.

Here is the message rewritten to appear on two lines: "Welcome!" & Chr(13) & Chr(10) & "Take your shoes off and stay a while."

used on your Web page. See the discussion earlier in this chapter for more information about help text.

Two additional arguments are necessary to offer on-line help to your visitor. These are the name of the file that contains the help text and the number of the topic that is to be displayed when the help file is accessed by the VB Script engine. This technique is illustrated in Example 9.8, as is the method for displaying a title for the message box dialog box.

Example 9.8 Adding a Title and Help to the Message Box Dialog Box

```
<SCRIPT LANGUAGE="VBS">
<!--

Dim intResponse

intResponse = MsgBox "Do you like my Web site?", 3, "Question",
persurvy", "23"

If intResponse = 6 Then
    MsgBox "I knew you'd like it.", 0, "Response")
Else
    MsgBox "I'd like to see you do better!", 0, "Response"
End If

-->
</SCRIPT>
```

NEXT TIME

What time is it? Do you know what year it is? No, this isn't a sanity test. However, you'll find a need to instruct the VB Script engine to answer these questions. Dates and time are kinds of information that must be treated uniquely by the VB Script engine.

The next chapter explores the various techniques that you can use to have the VB Script engine manipulate date and time information.

Missing Arguments

Throughout this chapter you've seen how we incrementally expanded the arguments to both the InputBox() and MsgBox() functions. This seems sensible as long as these arguments are used each time we use the function.

What happens if we want to use only some of these arguments? Well, you must be careful. First, you don't have to use all the arguments to these functions. You can use only those arguments that relate to the features you want to incorporate into the dialog box.

The trick is to keep the sequence of the arguments in order. For example, the third argument in the InputBox() function is always the default value. This means that you cannot use the name of the help file, or any other argument, as the third argument.

You can maintain the sequence of arguments by separating each argument with a comma, even if the argument value is left out. Here is a MsgBox() function that has all the argument values except for a title: MsgBox ("Do you like my Web site?", 3, "persurvy", "23"). Notice that the appropriate number of commas is used even when the value of the title argument is missing.

Chapter 10

Dates and Times

How About a Date?

Who signed the guest book today? How many visitors did you have over the past week? These are just some questions that you'll find yourself asking the VB Script engine. The VB Script engine can respond to your questions by following instructions that you give it in a VB Script. Those instructions must be able to tell the VB Script engine how to find the date information that you need. In the next few sections, we'll explore the techniques that you use to have the VB Script engine respond to those requests.

So, what's a date? Most of us think of a date as a series of formatted characters that are recognizable as a day on the calendar. When we enter date information into an editor or as a response to an InputBox() function, the information is stored as a string, a series of characters.

However, a date is more than a series of characters. A date is a subtype in the VB Script language that can be manipulated by the VB Script engine. For example, the VB Script engine can be told to subtract two dates to determine the number of days that transpired between them. This cannot be done with a string subtype.

We'll explore this difference in the next section. For now, let's simply ask the VB Script engine to tell us the current date. No, the VB Script engine doesn't need a calendar or a copy of today's newspaper. All the VB Script engine requires is the keyword Date().

By now you realize this is a call to the Date() function. This technique is illustrated in Example 10.1. Here, the VB Script engine assigns the date to the variable datToday, which is then displayed on the screen in a message box.

Example 10.1 Finding Today's Date

```
<SCRIPT LANGUAGE="VBS">
<!--
Dim datToday
datToday = Date()
MsgBox(datToday,0)
-->
</SCRIPT>
```

Where did the VB Script engine get the date? From your visitor's computer. Every computer has a built-in clock and software that keeps track of the date and time. This is called the *system's date* and is available to your VB Script by calling the Date() function.

When this function is called, the VB Script engine passes your request to the operating system—the software that makes your computer run. The operating system returns to the VB Script engine the current date and time of the internal clock. The VB Script engine then uses this information in your VB Script.

The date is returned in the format 12/25/1998. Later in this chapter you'll see how to have the VB Script engine take apart the date and even determine which day of the week it is.

A word of caution: Although your VB Script asks the VB Script engine to read the system's clock, you cannot assume that the date on the system's clock is correct. The system's date requires periodic maintenance and can be changed at any time—in most cases, by anyone who uses the computer. The exception is when the computer is connected to a network server. The system's clock on the server can be changed only by the system administrator, the person who is responsible for maintaining the network server.

YOU ARE NOW A DATE

When your visitor enters a date into an InputBox(), it is received as a string rather than a date. A date in the form of a string cannot be manipulated as a date by the VB Script engine. The VB Script engine requires that date information be stored as a date subtype; otherwise, the VB Script engine treats the date like any other string.

Confused? Remember the discussion about the difference between a string subtype and a numeric subtype in previous chapters. Variables of both subtypes can contain 1234. If the variable is a string subtype, then the 1234 is treated as a series of characters, each being independent of the others.

On the other hand, if the variable is a numeric subtype, then the 1234 is the number 1234 and each digit is considered related to the other digits and treated as a whole number. Therefore, you can use the number 1234 in calculation, whereas you cannot use the string 1234 in a calculation without first converting the string to a number.

The same principle holds true when dealing with a date. A date of 12/25/98 can be a string of characters that we recognize as a date or a date subtype that is recognized by the VB Script engine as a date. The date in the date subtype can be used in date calculations by the VB Script engine, which is something that cannot be done with the string version of the date.

A string form of a date can be converted to a date subtype by using the DateValue() function as shown in Example 10.2. A word of caution: The characters that are used to form the date in the string must conform to the standard convention of date formats; otherwise, the DateValue() function will not be able to convert the string subtype to a date subtype.

Example 10.2 Converting a String Subtype Date to a Date Subtype

```
<SCRIPT LANGUAGE="VBS">
<!--
Dim datToday
datToday = InputBox("Enter your birth date:")
If ( IsDate(datToday) ) then
    datToday = DateValue(datToday)
Else
    MsgBox("You must enter a valid date.",0)
End If
-->
</SCRIPT>
```

Before you tell the VB Script engine to perform the conversion, you should have the VB Script engine make sure that the conversion will be successful. You can do this by calling the IsDate() function in your script. This, too, is shown in Example 10.2.

The IsDate() function returns a value of True or False. In this example, if a True value is returned by the function, then the VB Script engine will convert the string version of the date to the date subtype. However, a False value causes the VB Script engine to skip the conversion process and display a message on the screen that informs the visitor that an inappropriate response was received.

CDate() is another conversion function you can use to change a string or a number into a date subtype. A date can be represented by a number, which will be seen later in this chapter. The CDate() converts any number within a valid date range to a date subtype.

Both the DateValue() and the CDate() functions recognize the date-formatted strings by the date format used by the system's date on the visitor's computer.

TAKING APART A DATE

Ready yourself for some date magic. The system's date or a date entered by a visitor into a text box is composed of three pieces of information: month, day, and year. You'll find that for some Web pages you create, the full date is just too much information. You really require only part of the date.

Perhaps you want the VB Script engine to know if two dates are within the same month. We showed you how to capture the date information. You also know how to compare values. But how do you break down the date into its various components?

Here's the trick. You can use three functions that instruct the VB Script engine to do the work for you. These are appropriately called Month(), Day(), and Year(). Each of these functions returns the numeric value within the component. That is, the Month() function will return a value between 1 and 12; the Day() function will return a value between 1 and 31; and the Year() function returns the whole number of the year.

Example 10.3 shows how each of these functions is used in a VB Script. First, the VB Script engine is told to get the system's date and assign the date to the datToday variable. This turns the datToday variable into a date subtype.

Example 10.3 Breaking a Date into Month, Day, and Year

```
<SCRIPT LANGUAGE="VBS">
<!--
Dim datToday, intMonth, intDay, intYear
datToday = Date()
intMonth = Month(datToday)
intDay = Day(datToday)
intYear = Year(datToday)
-->
</SCRIPT>
```

Next, the full date that is assigned to the datToday variable is passed as an argument to the Month() function. This returns an integer representing the corresponding number of the month. Likewise, the Day() function uses the datToday variable as an argument and returns the integer of the day of the month. Finally, the Year() function repeats the same sequence and returns the integer value of the year of the date.

Confused? Let's take a real-life example and see how this works. Today is 12-25-1998 (Merry Christmas!) according to the system clock of our computer. Thus, this is the date returned by the Date() function and assigned to the datToday variable.

Next, we let the VB Script engine determine the month by using the Month() function. The return value of this function is 12. Likewise, the Day() function returns 25, and the Year() function returns 1998.

Once the date is broken down into its components, you can use all the tricks that we've showed you throughout this book to reach a conclusion about the date. Example 10.4 illustrates one of these techniques.

Example 10.4 Using the Month to Reach a Decision

```
<SCRIPT LANGUAGE="VBS">
<!--
Dim datToday, intMonth
datToday = Date()
intMonth = Month(datToday)
If (intMonth > 5) then
   MsgBox "Your payment is late.",0
End If
-->
</SCRIPT>
```

Here, the Month() function is used to extract the month from the current system's date. The VB Script engine is then told to determine if the numeric equivalent of the month is greater than 5. In other words, is the current month after May? If this is true, then the visitor is told that the bill is overdue.

A word of caution: Remember that numeric values of months and days are not unique values. Every month has a day 15 and every year has a third month. Therefore, be careful when you use components of a date for comparisons. The results may not be what you expect. Let's say in Example 10.4 the month was January, the first month of the year. However, the year was next year. That bill was really overdue, but this VB Script won't notice it.

Example 10.5 shows you how to have the VB Script engine compare two dates. In this case, we created a datDueDate variable and used the DateVal() function to convert the literal string date into a date subtype. Next, we told the VB Script engine to compare both dates and, if datToday is greater than datDueDate, the VB Script engine is instructed to display the dunning notice on the screen in a message box.

Example 10.5 Comparing the Full Date

```
<SCRIPT LANGUAGE="VBS">
<!--
Dim datToday, datDueDate
datToday = Date()
datDueDate = DateValue("05/1/1998")
If (datToday > datDueDate) then
   MsgBox  "You're payment is late.",0
End If
-->
</SCRIPT>
```

ANOTHER WAY TO USE A DATE

Now that you've seen how to reduce a date into the numeric values of the date's month, day, and year, let's reverse this process. Let's take the numerical components of a date and have the VB Script engine convert those numbers into a valid date subtype.

We do this by using the DateSerial() function, as shown in Example 10.6. The DateSerial() function requires three arguments, which are the numeric values of the year, month, and day, in that order. This function converts the numeric values into the corresponding date, which, in this example, is assigned to the datToday variable.

Example 10.6 Recreating the Date from Numerical Components of a Date

```
<SCRIPT LANGUAGE="VBS">
<!--
Dim datToday, intMonth, intDay, intYear
datToday = Date()
intMonth = Month(datToday)
```

```
intDay = Day(datToday)
intYear = Year(datToday)
datToday = DateSerial(intYear, intMonth,intDay)
-->
</SCRIPT>
```

A word of caution: In addition to ensuring that the arguments are in the proper sequence, you must also be sure that the numeric values that are passed to the DateSerial() function are within the acceptable range for the component of the date. For example, the first argument (the year) must be an integer value between 100 and 9999, the second argument (the month) must be between the integer value 1 and 12, and the last argument (the day) must be between 1 and 31. An error will occur if any of the arguments is out of its appropriate range.

Here's a trick that you can perform with the DateSerial() function. You can specify a related year, month, and day in the argument rather than an explicit year, month, and day. Let's take this slowly and you'll quickly understand how to perform this trick.

Look at Example 10.6. Notice that in the DateSerial() function we specified a numeric value for a year, month, and day. Remember that these values are assigned to variables. This is an explicit method of passing components of a date to the DateSerial() function.

Now look at Example 10.7. This is practically the same VB Script, except the values of the arguments are implied by relating the value to another value. Take the first argument, for example. Here we tell the DateSerial() function that the year is actually 10 years earlier than the year specified by the number assigned to the intYear. If intYear has a value of 1998, then the value passed to the DateSerial() function would be 1988.

Example 10.7 Specifying a Relative Year, Month, and Day

```
<SCRIPT LANGUAGE="VBS">
<!--
Dim datToday, intMonth, intDay, intYear
datToday = Date()
intMonth = Month(datToday)
intDay = Day(datToday)
intYear = Year(datToday)
```

```
datToday = DateSerial(intYear - 10, intMonth + 4, intDay - 6)
-->
</SCRIPT>
```

Likewise, the same technique is used to specify the month and day. In the case of the month, we told the DateSerial() function to use a month that is four months from now. If this month is February, then the second argument in the DateSerial() function is 6 (June). And the day is six days ago.

WHAT DAY OF THE WEEK IS IT?

Your VB Script is smart enough to know the day of the week—by using the proper function, that is. The function is WeekDay(). The WeekDay() function requires one argument but can accept another one, as you will see.

The first argument to the function is the date. This is shown in Example 10.8. The WeekDay() function translates the date into the number that represents the day of the week. Once this number is known, we can write the necessary instructions to translate the day of the week into English.

Example 10.8 Identifying the Day of the Week of a Date

```
<SCRIPT LANGUAGE="VBS">
<!--
Dim datToday, intWeekDay
datToday = Date()
intWeekDay = WeekDay(datToday)
Select Case intWeekDay

CaseVB Sunday
    MsgBox "Sunday",0
CaseVB Monday
    MsgBox "Monday",0
CaseVB Tuesday
    MsgBox "Tuesday",0
CaseVB Wednesday
    MsgBox "Wednesday",0
```

```
CaseVB Thursday
    MsgBox "Thursday",0
CaseVB Friday
    MsgBox "Friday",0
CaseVB Saturday
    MsgBox "Saturday",0
End Select

-->
</SCRIPT>
```

Note that in this example, the Select Case statement—something you learned about earlier in the book—matches the integer returned by the WeekDay() function against the numbers that correspond to the days of the week. Beneath each Case keyword is the instruction that tells the VB Script engine to display a message box with the corresponding message.

Wait, there are no numbers. The names of the days of the week are constants. You may remember that a constant is a series of characters, not a string, used to represent a value that doesn't change when the VB Script is executed. Table 10.1 contains a list of constants, their corresponding numeric values, and their meanings. You can use either the constant or the numeric value within the Select Case statement.

Here's a test. Can you rewrite the VB Script in Example 10.8 so that only a single MsgBox() function is used?

How about the second argument? We're getting to that, but before we do, here's another question: What is the first day of the week? You'll need to know the answer to this question before you specify the second argument to the WeekDay() function.

Table 10.1 Return Values of the Weekend( ) Function

Value	*Description*
1	Sunday
2	Monday
3	Tuesday
4	Wednesday
5	Thursday
6	Friday
7	Saturday

Sunday is the first day of the week. No, Monday is. Both answers are correct. According to the WeekDay() function, any day can be the first day of the week. You specify which day of the week is the first one by using the value or constant shown in Table 10.1 as the second argument to the WeekDay() function.

Hint: You can avoid specifying a different first day of the week. The traditional first day is Sunday, which is the default setting of the WeekDay() function. Most visitors to your Web site will expect Sunday as the first day. Any other day might be confusing.

DO YOU HAVE THE TIME?

What time is it? This sounds like the opening of a favorite children's program. You can ask this question in the form of an instruction to the VB Script engine and the response you'll receive will be right on the mark—almost.

The Time() function is used to determine the current time according to the system's clock of the visitor's computer. This technique is shown in Example 10.9. The accuracy of the time is to the second, assuming that the system's clock is set to the proper time. If not, then your VB Script cannot depend on the value returned by the Time() function.

Example 10.9 Finding the Current Time

```
<SCRIPT LANGUAGE="VBS">
<!--
Dim tmTime
tmTime = Time()
MsgBox tmTime,0
-->
</SCRIPT>
```

What if your visitor's computer is in a time zone where the clocks are moved ahead an hour every spring? You can bet that all the time pieces in the house are adjusted, but you can't say the same about the system's clock on the visitor's computer. You can't avoid this problem whenever you use the Time() function.

In Example 10.9, the value returned by the Time() function is assigned to the tmTime variable, making it a time subtype. The format of the time is in hours:minutes:seconds and reflects the format used on the visitor's system's clock.

If capturing the correct time is important to your VB Script and you cannot be sure that the system's clock is properly adjusted, the next best thing to do is to ask the visitor for the time. The value entered by the visitor is a string and must be converted to a time subtype. This is shown in Example 10.10.

Example 10.10 Converting a String Subtype Time to a Time Subtype

```
<SCRIPT LANGUAGE="VBS">
<!--
Dim tmTime
tmTime = InputBox("Enter the current time:")
tmTime = TimeValue(tmTime)
-->
</SCRIPT>
```

Here the TimeVal() function is used for the conversion. First, the InputBox() function is used to capture the new time from the visitor, which is assigned to the tmTime variable. Next, the VB Script engine is told to convert this information into the proper subtype and assign the results to the tmTime variable. Remember, a reassignment of a value to a variable overwrites the previous value that is assigned to the variable.

Hold on! There are two formats that can be used to enter time. There is the 24-hour (military) time format or the AM and PM time format. For example, 14:00:00 and 2:00:00 PM are the same time. The first time is in the 24-hour time format and the second time is in the PM time format.

Which time format can be used with the TimeVal() function? Both formats are acceptable. The TimeVal() function is smart enough to figure which time format is being used, then will make the necessary adjustments when converting the string to the time subtype.

TAKING APART TIME

As with a date, you might need to reference a portion of the full time. You could be interested in only the seconds of the current time rather than the hours and minutes.

You can get this portion of the time by picking apart just the piece that you need. You do this by saying the magic words Second(), Minute(), and Hour().

Example 10.11 shows how to dissect the return value by the Time() function. First, the time from the system's clock is retrieved and assigned to the tmTime variable. Next, the VB Script engine is told to extract the seconds, minutes, and hours from this variable. Note that the tmTime variable is passed as the argument to the Second(), Minute(), and Hour() functions.

Example 10.11 Breaking a Time into Seconds, Minutes, and Hours

```
<SCRIPT LANGUAGE="VBS">
<!--
Dim tmTime, intSecond, intMinute, intHour
tmTime = Time()
intSecond = Second(tmTime)
intMinute = Minute(tmTime)
intHour = Hour(tmTime)
-->
</SCRIPT>
```

Each of these functions returns an integer that represents the corresponding segment of the time and assigns this value to the related variable. Seconds and minutes are reported as integer values between 0 and 59. Hours are reported as integer values between 0 and 23.

A word of caution: Regardless of the time format of the argument passed to the Hour() function, the results are always reported in the 24-hour time format. That is, the hour between 12 midnight and 1 AM is reported as the integer 0.

ANOTHER WAY TO LOOK AT TIME

If we can break down time into integers, you probably suspect that we can reverse the process by assembling integers back into a time subtype. And you'd be correct. The function that does this for us is the TimeSerial() function.

The TimeSerial() function, shown in Example 10.12, requires that the hour, minute, and second integers of the time be passed as arguments to this function. These values are then converted into a proper time subtype and returned by TimeSerial(), which is assigned to the tmTime variable.

Example 10.12 Recreating the Time from Numerical Components

```
<SCRIPT LANGUAGE="VBS">
<!--
Dim tmTime, intSecond, intMinute, intHour
tmTime = Time()
intSecond = Second(tmTime)
intMinute = Minute(tmTime)
intHour = Hour(tmTime)
tmTime = TimeSerial(intHour, intMinute, intSecond)
-->
</SCRIPT>
```

Be careful when you use this function. The arguments must be in the proper order and within the proper ranges for the segment of time. That is, hours, minutes, and seconds, each separated by a comma, is the only order in which the arguments can be passed to the function. The integer range for the hour argument must be between 0 and 23, while both the minutes and seconds must be integer values between 0 and 59. Any deviation from this sequence will cause a recalculation.

However, you can imply the hour, minute, and second values in the argument. This technique is shown in Example 10.13. The implied argument requires that the function use the expression in the argument to determine the correct value. In this example, the first argument instructs the TimeSerial() function to subtract two hours from the value of the intHour variable, then convert this value into a time subtype.

Likewise, 30 minutes is added to the current value of the intMinute variable and 40 seconds is subtracted from the intSecond variable before these values are converted by the TimeSerial() function.

Example 10.13 Specifying a Relative Hour, Minute, and Second

```
<SCRIPT LANGUAGE="VBS">
<!--
Dim tmTime, intSecond, intMinute, intHour
tmTime = Time()
intSecond = Second(tmTime)
intMinute = Minute(tmTime)
intHour = Hour(tmTime)
tmTime = TimeSerial(intHour - 2, intMinute + 30, intSecond - 40)
-->
</SCRIPT>
```

NEXT TIME

By now you have a pretty good understanding of how to create a VB Script and make it perform magic for your Web site, but something is missing. Where are all the dramatic tricks that make it worth your while to learn the VB Script language?

The techno jargon for what you are looking for is an *object*. You know these as radio buttons, list boxes, check boxes—the list is nearly endless. These are the things that give your Web page the professional look your visitors expect when they visit your site.

Well, the time is almost here for you to learn how to use these objects in your VB Script. You'll learn all about them in the next chapter.

Chapter 11

VB Scripts and Objects

The Object Of Objects

Did you ever want to dip into someone else's program and make it part of your VB Script? Let's say that you see this neat application, Excel, and you want to use a piece of it to enhance the performance of your Web page. This seems like a dream. How can you tap into such power without being a computer wiz and without getting caught by Microsoft?

It's not that difficult, thanks to Microsoft's *Object Linking and Embedding (OLE)*, which is now called *Active X control*. And after you've used it a few times you'll be shouting "OLE"! OLE is a technology pioneered by Microsoft that enables your HTML code to use data from an assortment of applications and to edit the data using the application. And once the link is made to your Web page, you can use VB Script to interact with the object.

The data is supplied by the Active X control application and is called an *Active X object*. In the case of Excel, the Active X object can be a worksheet, a chart, a cell, or a range of cells. Each is a separate object. Later in this chapter, you'll learn how to use an HTML language tag to create a link to an object and embed the object into your Web page.

Before you begin thinking how you are going to incorporate objects from another application into your Web page, we'd better break some bad news to you. Applications that provide objects that support Active X controls are the only applications that can be linked to your Web page.

Here's how Active X control works. Your Web page links to the object by using the <OBJECT> tag to reference the object's identification number. This makes your Web page a *container application*, which is an application that contains an *Active X link*.

A snapshot of the data is then made available to your Web page. For example, if you embed an Excel spreadsheet, all the data associated with the cells of the spreadsheet, including any formulas in the cells, are available to your Web page. And when the object is embedded, other applications cannot have access to the data.

USING ACTIVE X OBJECTS

Applications that give your Web page access to objects of the application through the use of Active X are said to be in compliance with the OLE automation industry standard. Therefore, a spreadsheet like Excel is said to be an Active X application, as are most Microsoft products, including Word for Windows. Products produced by other manufacturers can also be Active X applications.

Each Active X application has different Active X objects that can be exposed to your Web page and other Active X applications. We mentioned that cells in a spreadsheet are accessible to your Web page, and so are objects of a word processor. These include a full document or a particular paragraph or sentence of the document.

Once your Web page has linked with the Active X object, your Web page can manipulate the object by setting the properties of the object. A *property* consists of one or more characteristics or behaviors that define the object.

Sounds like more techno jargon. However, this is one time when the formal definition of a term doesn't do much justice to its meaning. The property is an object's characteristic, such as its size, color, screen location, or other features like whether or not the object is visible or enabled.

Another way of using an object is to call an object's method. A *method* is a procedure or function that does something with the object. This differs from other procedures and functions used in a VB Script in that methods are part of the Active X application and not part of your VB Script. Furthermore, they affect only the object that is linked to your Web page. This means you cannot use a method associated with an Active X object with any other object.

If you're confused, Example 11.1 will probably set you straight. For this illustration, assume that your Web page has already linked to the Active X object and that the reference to the Active X object is identified as FirstName. We'll show you how this is done later in this chapter. FirstName is really a variable of *object subtype*.

We use the object variable any time we want to refer to the Active X object in our VB Script. Properties and methods of the Active X object are associated with the object variable by using the dot operator. This is shown in the three statements in the VB Script in this example. The first statement calls the Insert method, which places the string "Bob" in the Active X object, which could be a word processing document.

The next statement changes the characteristic of the Active X object by making the text appear in bold characters. Finally, the last statement calls another Active X method of the object that saves the document as a particular file name.

Notice that the Insert and the SaveAs methods perform actions with no need for your VB Script to give additional instructions. In the first instance, the Insert method knows how to place the string "Bob" into the document; additional instructions are not required. Likewise, the SaveAs method knows how to save the document to disk. All your VB Script needs to do is to link with the proper Active X object and call the appropriate method.

Example 11.1 Properties and Methods of an Object

```
FirstName.Insert "Bob"
FirstName.Bold
FirstName.SaveAs "c:\data\names.doc"
```

OVERCOMING INHERENT HURDLES

Using Active X objects with your Web page sounds like a no brainer. All that you need to do is to use the <OBJECT> tag in the HTML language, which you'll learn how to do later in this chapter, then set the properties of the Active X object. Don't be too quick. You must do a few things before using an Active X object in your Web page.

Let's begin with the properties and methods associated with the Active X object. In Example 11.1 you saw the proper syntax for setting a property and calling a method. However, how do you know which properties and methods exist? You don't unless you do your homework.

The properties and methods used with an Active X object are defined by the application that owns the object and not the VB Script or HTML language. In the previous example, the SaveAs method is part of the word processor software that made available the document object to our Web page.

How do you know about these properties and methods? You must refer to the documentation that comes with the application that owns the Active X object. This is the only way to be sure that the property or method used in your Web page for the Active X object will actually work.

The next problem with working with Active X objects is that you must be sure that the Active X object exists on the computer running your Web page. If not, then there is no way for your Web page to use the Active X object. The Active X object simply doesn't exist and, therefore, cannot be linked to by your Web page.

The best way to solve this problem is to use Active X objects that are owned by the most common applications. Next, present the visitor with a menu asking the visitor which applications are available on the visitor's computer. Store the response in a variable that can be used with a decision statement (i.e., If Then) to determine what Active X objects can be used in your Web page.

Of course, you must determine the properties and methods available to those Active X objects, then build in those settings within the Web page. Let's say that the visitor selected Microsoft Word for Windows as the word processor running on his or her computer. Your Web page must contain the statements necessary to access and work with an Active X object that is owned by Microsoft Word for Windows.

And another hurdle you must overcome before your Web page can utilize an Active X object is that the visitor's browser must be an Active X control browser, such as the Microsoft Internet Explorer. Various dynamic linking libraries are loaded onto the visitor's computer when the browser is installed. These libraries are necessary for Active X to work.

ACTIVE X OBJECTS AND THE BROWSER

Although we've been talking about using an Active X object owned by another application, such as Excel or Word For Windows, Active X objects also exist within the browser itself. Once the object is created, your VB Script can access the object and modify its properties, the results of which appear immediately on the browser.

Let's take a closer look and see how this is done. Example 11.2 shows a Web page that allows the visitor to change the caption property of an object. The Web page is divided into three components: a label object, a form, and a VB Script. The label object is defined with the <OBJECT> tag. This object is one found in the Microsoft Internet Explorer. Note that the object is identified by a *class identifier* (classid), which is an internal reference to the Microsoft Internet Explorer. You must refer to the Microsoft Internet Explorer documentation for a complete listing of the identifiers, properties, and methods.

The next statement defines the identifier lblActiveLbl used within the Web page to refer to the object. Other statements in this section define how the object appears on the screen. The <PARAM> tag is used to define property settings for the object. The properties shown here are for the label object. Each object and each application that owns the object has a unique list of properties. Here we set the caption, the font, and the size of the character for the object.

A form is then created that displays a text input box and a button titled "Change Text." The Web page waits for the visitor to enter text, which is assigned to the txtNewText variable. When the visitor presses the Change Text button, the browser executes the VB Script.

The VB Script defines a variable that is assigned the reference to the form. The text value of the txtNewText variable is assigned to the caption property of the object lblActiveLbl.Caption. This changes the caption to any text entered by the visitor.

Example 11.2 Using an Active X Object and a Form with a VB Script

```
<HTML>
<BODY>

<OBJECT
    classid="clsid:99B42120-6EC7-11CF-A6C7-00AA00A47DD2"
    id=lblActiveLbl
    width=225
    height=225
    align=left
    hspace=25
    vspace=0
>
<PARAM NAME="Caption" VALUE="Your First Name">
<PARAM NAME="FontName" VALUE="Arial">
<PARAM NAME="FontSize" VALUE="20">
<PARAM NAME="FontBold" VALUE="1">
</OBJECT>

<FORM NAME="LabelControls">
<INPUT TYPE="TEXT" NAME="txtNewText" SIZE=25>
<INPUT TYPE="BUTTON" NAME="cmdChangeIt" VALUE="Change Text">
</FORM>

<SCRIPT LANGUAGE="VBS">
<!--
Sub cmdChangeIt_onClick
    Dim MyForm
    Set MyForm = Document.LabelControls
    lblActiveLbl.Caption = MyForm.txtNewText.Value
End Sub
-->
</SCRIPT>

</BODY>
</HTML>
```

We used a few new VB Script language conventions in this example. Let's step through the VB Script to become acquainted with the new syntax. The VB Script contains a procedure that is automatically called by the VB Script engine when the visitor clicks on the cmdChangeIt button.

The first statement within the procedure declares a variable called MyForm. The Set statement is used to assign the document called LabelControls to the MyForm variable, making this an object subtype.

The next statement tells the VB Script engine to locate the value of the txtNewText variable on the form that is pointed to by the MyForm variable. Each of these keywords must be separated by the dot operator. The assignment operator (=) is then used to assign this value to the caption property of the object that is pointed to by the lblActiveLbl identifier. Again, the dot operator must separate the identifier from the property.

Although this example illustrates the technique for accessing an object of the Microsoft Internet Explorer, a similar technique can be used for any browser that supports Active X controls. That is, you must review the documentation of the applications that owns the object to learn how to properly identify the object, properties, and methods.

ACTIVE X OBJECTS AND ANIMATION

Active X is also a way for you to add animation to your Web site. You'll need to find an Active X animation control that is a component of another Active X application such as Visual Basic.

The animation control must be available to your Web page. This means the control itself needs to be placed on your Web server or on your vistor'e computer. The best bet is to store the control on your Web server. This will ensure that your Web page will always know where to find it. Consult with your Web server provider on how to place the animation control or other Active X controls that you need onto the Web server.

You link the animation control to your Web page using the <OBJECT> tag and the rest of the technique described in this chapter. After the link to the animation control is made, you can modify the control's properties and call the control's methods, as also shown in this chapter.

What are properties and methods? How do you modify the properties and call the methods? We've already shown how to change the property of an Active X control and call its method. The same technique is employed when using an animation control.

The properties and methods that you'll be working withdepend on the animation control that is linked to your Web page. You must consult the documentation (usually on-line help) that is associated with the animation control to identify the control's properties and methods.

WHAT NEXT?

The end is in sight. You have almost completed your adventure into the VB Script language. Next, we'll look at how to relate components of your Visual Basic applications to everything presented in this book. After you're finished, you will be able to convert many of your Visual Basic applications to your Web site by using a combination of VB Script language and HTML language.

Chapter 12

Converting Visual Basic to VB Script

The Dissection of a Visual Basic Application

Now it is time to use many of the tricks that are presented in previous chapters and explore a simple way to convert a typical Visual Basic application into a VB Script application. Let's begin by dissecting a Visual Basic application.

A Visual Basic application is composed of one or more forms. Each form contains controls. A *control* is a text box, radio button, check box, or some other button—the list is nearly endless thanks to programmers who create new controls that can be purchased in the secondary marketplace.

Each control has specific characteristics and behavior. A control *characteristic* is determined by a property setting. For example, a text box control has a property called *font*, and the value that is assigned to the font property determines the font used to display the text within the control.

The behavior of a control falls into two categories: those behaviors that are inherent and those that are customized. An *inherent behavior* is one already built into the control, such as an X displayed in a check box when the control is selected. A *customized behavior* is one you instruct the computer to perform, using the Visual Basic programming language. An example of a customized behavior is a command button control that executes instructions you wrote.

The customized behavior of a control is associated with an event. Numerous kinds of events occur. A click or select event is just one. Some others include pressing the right mouse button, placing the cursor over the control (control receives focus), and moving the cursor away from the control (control loses focus).

The instructions you provide to react to an event are placed in a procedure linked to an event for a particular control. Collectively, these procedures are called the *methods* for the control.

Many kinds of controls are available in Visual Basic. Most of these controls are provided with the product; others are offered in the secondary market as VBX libraries. A *library* is a file containing groups of procedures and function procedures that can be used in an application. These libraries allow the Visual Basic application to perform fancy tricks, such as communicating with other computers via a modem.

DIFFERENCES BETWEEN VISUAL BASIC AND VB SCRIPT

If you're not a Visual Basic programmer, then the previous section is bound to confuse you. I recommend that you brush up on your Visual

Basic programming before proceeding with the rest of this chapter. However, if you're still on track, then let's see how building a VB Script application differs from that of a Visual Basic application.

Probably the outstanding difference between these two kinds of application language is that the VB Script language is linked in scope and therefore must blend with other languages to create the final application. Simply put, other languages are better suited to perform specific functions than the VB Script language.

For example, HTML is an ideal language to use to display controls on the screen and collect information from your visitor. This is because the visitor's browser knows how to interpret the HTML code in a way that is acceptable to the visitor's computer. Basically, the browser knows how to display a radio button—you just have to give it appropriate information about the button.

However, the VB Script language is more powerful than HTML when it comes to manipulating the information entered by a visitor. Therefore, you can use the VB Script language to read information that was collected by HTML. You'll learn this technique later in this chapter.

If you're familiar with HTML and Visual Basic, you realize that HTML contains only a limited number of controls when compared to Visual Basic. For example, you have no communication control in HTML, nor do you have those fancy controls in VB Script. How do you overcome this limitation? You do so by blending in another application with the VB Script application. This is accomplished by linking the VB Script to an Active X object owned by an application that can offer the control you require. This technique was discussed in the previous chapter.

A word of caution: Remember that you are working on the Internet. Inherent limitations of that environment make many of the fancy controls found in Visual Basic useless in the VB Script application. The communications control is a perfect example. A visitor to your Web site probably has only one modem attached to his or her computer, and that one is being used to connect to your Web site. Therefore, it makes no sense to have a communications control in your VB Script application.

However, remember that some of these fancy controls, such as those that give sound and video capabilities to your Visual Basic application, are available by using HTML to have the visitor's browser call the appropriate audio or video player.

Here are a few points to remember when converting your Visual Basic application to a VB Script application:

- Expect to use HTML, VB Script, and maybe an Active X linked object to make the VB Script application perform like your Visual Basic application.
- The VB Script application is limited by the Internet environment and the interpretation of HTML by the visitor's browser. In contrast, the Visual Basic application is limited only by your Visual Basic programming skills.
- Not all the controls used in the Visual Basic application are available or useful with the VB Script application.
- Match the controls in your Visual Basic application with those that are available with HTML. Re-create the methods for those controls in the VB Script.

Matching Text Box Controls

We begin our matching of controls with the text box control. This is the control used to accept free-form text from the user of the application. In a Visual Basic application, you use the text box control. In the VB Script application, you have two choices. You can use an InputBox() function, as described previously, or you can use HTML. I recommend that you use HTML, since your application probably combines other controls with the text box control.

There are two kinds of text box controls: a single-line entry and a multiple-line entry. The single-line entry, shown in Example 12.1, prompts a visitor to your Web site to enter his or her name. You'll notice that this control has several properties, called *attributes*. These attributes tell the browser how to use the control.

Example 12.1 Single-Line Text Box Control

```
<FORM>
<P> Enter Your Name:
<INPUT TYPE="TEXT" NAME="Name" SIZE="30" MAXLENGTH="30">
</P>
<INPUT TYPE="BUTTON" NAME="cmdFinished" VALUE="Finished">
```

```
<INPUT TYPE="BUTTON" NAME="cmdCancel" VALUE="Cancel">
</FORM>
```

The <INPUT> tag instructs the browser to read information supplied by the visitor. The TYPE attribute defines the text box control that the browser needs to display on the Web page. The NAME attribute gives the control a unique identifier, which is used by the VB Script. The VB Script isn't shown in this example but will be contained in Example 12.7, later in this chapter.

The SIZE attribute tells the browser that the text box must be wide enough to contain up to 30 characters. A visitor can enter more than 30 characters, but only the first 30 characters are shown. The remaining characters are displayed by scrolling to the right.

The MAXLENGTH attribute limits the number of characters that can be entered into the text box control by the visitor. In this example, both the SIZE and the MAXLENGTH attributes are set to the same value. This causes the browser to display sufficient room on the screen for the maximum number of characters that a visitor can enter into the control.

The SIZE value has a 20-character default setting, so if you fail to set a SIZE value, the browser automatically will provide enough space for 20 characters. It is recommended that you keep the value of the SIZE attribute under 50 characters. This will ensure sufficient room on the screen to display the text box control.

A word of caution: Some browsers use the MAXLENGTH attribute value to override the SIZE attribute value whenever the MAXLENGTH value is greater than the SIZE attribute value.

Visual Basic applications can allow a visitor to enter multiple lines of text in a text box. You can do the same within HTML by using <TEXTAREA>. This is illustrated in Example 12.2, where a visitor is asked to enter general comments.

There are three attributes for <TEXTAREA>: NAME, which contains the unique name of the control; ROW, which specifies the number of lines of text that can be entered into the text area; and COLS, which specifies the number of characters that can be on each line. A text area can have a maximum of 255 characters in total.

Example 12.2 Multiple-Line Text Box Control

```
<FORM>
<P> Enter Your Comments:
<TEXTAREA NAME="Comments" ROW="15" COLS="60">
</TEXTAREA>
</P>
<INPUT TYPE="BUTTON" NAME="cmdFinished" VALUE="Finished">
<INPUT TYPE="BUTTON" NAME="cmdCancel" VALUE="Cancel">
</FORM>
```

Just as in a Visual Basic application, the information entered into the text box control remains displayed until a visitor selects the appropriate command button control. Once the selection is made, the text is assigned to the name of the text box control and is made available to other parts of the Web page, including the VB Script. You'll see how to capture this information later in this chapter.

Matching Drop-Down List Controls

A feature in many Visual Basic applications is that the user is provided with a choice of acceptable options to select from a list. This helps the user better understand what information the programmer expects to receive.

HTML offers a similar drop-down list control that can be substituted for the drop-down list control found in Visual Basic applications. In HTML, this is presented as options to the <SELECT> tag, as shown in Example 12.3. Here, a visitor to the Web site is asked to pick the color of his or her hair from a drop-down list.

<SELECT> has two attributes in this example: NAME, which is the unique name used to identify the control on the Web page; and OPTION, which is used to identify each item that appears on the drop-down list.

Example 12.3 A Single-Selection Drop-down List Box

```
<FORM>
<P> Hair color:
<SELECT NAME="haircolor">
<OPTION>Brown
```

```
<OPTION>Black
<OPTION>BLonde
<OPTION>Red
<OPTION>Gray
</SELECT></P>
<INPUT TYPE="BUTTON" NAME="cmdFinished" VALUE="Finished">
<INPUT TYPE="BUTTON" NAME="cmdCancel" VALUE="Cancel">
</FORM>
```

A visitor can select only one item from the list. Once an item is selected, the previously selected item on the list is overridden. This works very similar to a radio button control. However, more than one selection can be made by using the MULTIPLE attribute, as illustrated in Example 12.4.

Example 12.4 A Multiple-Selection Drop-Down List Box

```
<FORM>
<P> Degrees:
<SELECT NAME="degrees" MULTIPLE SIZE=3>
<OPTION>BS
<OPTION>BA
<OPTION>MS
<OPTION>MBA
<OPTION>MA
<OPTION>PhD
</SELECT></P>
<INPUT TYPE="BUTTON" NAME="cmdFinished" VALUE="Finished">
<INPUT TYPE="BUTTON" NAME="cmdCancel" VALUE="Cancel">
</FORM>
```

You'll also notice in this example that the SIZE attribute is used and set to a value of 3. The SIZE attribute tells the browser how many items to display in the drop-down list box. Here, only three items are displayed. The remaining items can be accessed by using the vertical scroll bar that automatically appears in the drop-down list box. The SIZE attribute can be used with or without the MULTIPLE attribute.

When a visitor presses the command button, the text of the selected item on the drop-down list is assigned to the name of the control and made available to other parts of the Web page. Later, you'll see how to read this value by using your VB Script.

A word of caution: If multiple values are selected, then each selection is concatenated to the other and the entire string of text is assigned to the name of the drop-down list control. This means that your VB Script must have the logic to separate this long string of text into individual selections.

Sound like a tough job? It isn't. Each selection is separated by a hash sign. Therefore, you can use a loop and If Then statement to break down the string of text into each selection. Review the chapters on loops and If then statements before attempting this technique in your VB Script.

Matching Radio Button Controls

Radio buttons can be created easily in your VB Script application by using the <INPUT> tag with the TYPE attribute set with a value of "radio". This is shown in Example 12.5. The trick with using radio buttons is to have the browser recognize each radio button as a member of a unique group of radio buttons on the Web page.

Example 12.5 Creating Radio Buttons

```
<FORM>
<OL>
<INPUT TYPE="radio" NAME="GroupOne"  VALUE="Male">Male
<INPUT TYPE="radio" NAME=" GroupOne"  VALUE=" Female">Female
</OL>
<INPUT TYPE="BUTTON" NAME="cmdFinished" VALUE="Finished">
<INPUT TYPE="BUTTON" NAME="cmdCancel" VALUE="Cancel">
</FORM>
```

The solution to this problem is in the value of the NAME attribute. Note in this example that each radio button statement contains the same name, "GroupOne". Radio buttons that have the same name are treated as members of the same group.

When a visitor to the Web site selects one of the radio buttons within the group, the browser automatically unselects all the other radio buttons in the group. Just a note: Although the radio button name in this example is called GroupOne, you can use any unique name to identify the name of the radio button group.

Each radio button also has a VALUE attribute, which is the text assigned to the name of the radio button group when a visitor to your Web site selects the appropriate command button on the Web page. Remember, only one of those values in the radio button group is available to your VB Script.

You'll also notice that the text of the value appears at the end of each <INPUT> tag statement. Text outside the greater than (>) symbol is the label for the radio button. Although both the value and the label are the same here, they can be different and have no effect on each other. The label appears on the Web page, and the value is available to your VB Script.

Matching Check Box Controls

A check box is another common control that you probably use in a VB Script application. This control enables the user of the application to have the computer place an X in a box that is associated with an option.

HTML can help your VB Script application create a check box on your Web page by assigning the "checkbox" value to the TYPE attribute of the <INPUT> tag. You'll notice in Example 12.6 that the syntax for creating a check box is very similar to the statement used to create a radio button.

Example 12.6 Creating Check Boxes

```
<FORM>
<UL>
<LI><INPUT TYPE="checkbox" NAME ="BS" VALUE="checked">BS
<LI><INPUT TYPE="checkbox" NAME ="MS" VALUE="checked">MS
<LI><INPUT TYPE="checkbox" NAME ="PhD" VALUE="checked">PhD
</UL>
<INPUT TYPE="BUTTON" NAME="cmdFinished" VALUE="Finished">
<INPUT TYPE="BUTTON" NAME="cmdCancel" VALUE="Cancel">
</FORM>
```

In this case, the NAME attributes contain unique names of the check boxes, and the VALUE attributes are assigned the same value, called "checked". The name of each check box must be unique, since each is treated independent of the others, unlike radio buttons.

Although "checked" is used as the value for each check box, you are free to use any value. Keep in mind that the value of a check box is either true or false. That is, either a visitor to your Web site selected the check box or did not. Therefore, the value "checked" is sufficient to tell your VB Script that the check box is selected.

Each check box has a label that identifies the meaning of the selection to the visitor. This description, like the radio button, is the text that appears at the end of the check box statement. In many cases, the description is the same text as the name of the check box. This makes it easier for you to work with the data within the VB Script.

When a visitor selects the command button, values of all the check boxes are assigned to their appropriate names and are made available to your VB Script. You can determine which check boxes were selected by using the Len() function. As you may recall, the Len() function returns the length of a string; in this case, the length of the value assigned to the name of the check box. If the Len() function returns a value of 0, then your VB Script knows that a visitor did not select the check box.

You can combine the return value of the Len() function with the If Then statement to have the VB Script engine execute just the portion of the VB Script that will use a selected check box. This statement will also cause the VB Script engine to ignore unselected check boxes.

LINKING HTML WITH YOUR VB SCRIPT

Throughout this chapter we've talked about how to recreate common controls used in Visual Basic applications with in a VB Script application. Not all the controls in Visual Basic have a comparable set of controls in HTML and VB Script. Therefore, you may find it necessary to modify the capabilities of your Visual Basic application when converting it to a VB Script application.

Now let's see how your VB Script can gain access to the information collected by HTML. Example 12.7 shows how to build a Web page that contains a blend of HTML and a VB Script. Several kinds of controls are used on the page: a single-line text box, radio buttons, check boxes, a drop-down list box, a multiline text box, and a command button. All of these controls are contained on a form.

Example 12.7 Using a Form with a VB Script

```
<HTML>
<BODY>

<FORM NAME="CommentForm">

<P> Enter Your Name:
<INPUT TYPE=TEXT" NAME="Name" SIZE="30" MAXLENGTH="30">
</P>

<OL>
<INPUT TYPE="radio" NAME="GroupOne"  VALUE="Male">Male
<INPUT TYPE="radio" NAME="GroupOne"  VALUE="Female">Female
</OL>

<UL>
<LI><INPUT TYPE="checkbox" NAME ="BS" VALUE="checked">BS
<LI><INPUT TYPE="checkbox" NAME ="MS" VALUE="checked">MS
<LI><INPUT TYPE="checkbox" NAME ="PhD" VALUE="checked">PhD
</UL>

<P> Hair color:
<SELECT NAME="haircolor">
<OPTION>Brown
<OPTION>Black
<OPTION>BLonde
<OPTION>Red
<OPTION>Gray
</SELECT></P>

<P> Enter Your Comments:
<TEXTAREA NAME="Comments" ROW="15" COLS="60">
<TEXTAREA>
</P>

<INPUT TYPE="BUTTON" NAME="cmdFinished" VALUE="Finished">
<INPUT TYPE="BUTTON" NAME="cmdCancel" VALUE="Cancel">

</FORM>

<SCRIPT LANGUAGE="VBS">
<!--
Sub cmdFinished_onClick

    Dim MyForm ,Visitor, Sex, Degree1, Degree2, Degree3, Hair
    Set MyForm = Document.CommentForm
    Visitor = MyForm.Name.Value
    Sex = MyForm.GroupOne.Value
```

```
    Degree1 = MyForm.BS.Value
    Degree2 = MyForm.MS.Value
    Degree3 = MyForm.PhD.Value
    Hair = MyForm.HairColor.Value
End Sub
-->
</SCRIPT>

</BODY>
</HTML>
```

The previous sections showed how to use these controls. Now we'll turn our attention to learning how to read the input gathered by the controls, using a VB Script. The VB Script, shown in the last half of Example 12.7, consists of a procedure called cmdFinished_onClick.

When a visitor clicks on the cmdFinished command button on the form, the browser immediately starts the VB Script engine that reads this procedure. However, this procedure would be skipped if a visitor selected the Cancel command button on the form.

The procedure begins by declaring several variables. The first variable, MyForm, is assigned the reference to the HTML form called CommentForm. Each time we want the VB Script engine to refer to a control on the HTML form, we use the MyForm variable. Remember, you can call this variable anything as long as it is a valid variable name.

All the other variables are assigned the return values of their respective HTML controls from the form. The values are referenced within the VB Script by using the variables that reference the form, the names of the controls as they appear on the form, and the Value properties for the control.

Once a value is assigned to a VB Script variable, then you can use it as you would any variable in a VB Script. You've seen many examples of this throughout this book. However, the value returned by the HTML control contains both the name of the control and the value in a single text string. This means that your VB Script must strip away the name of the control before its value can be used by your script. A technique for doing this is shown in the following box.

Parsing Return Values

An HTML control value ends up as the name of the control followed by an equal sign, then the text that a visitor entered into the control or the text assigned to the VALUE attribute of the control.

For example, say we have a text box control called Name, which is used to collect the name of a visitor to our Web site. When a visitor presses the command button, the value that is available to other parts of the HTML Web page, including the VB Script, is "Name=Natalie." This assumes that the visitor's name is Natalie. The quotation marks are not part of the value.

Your job is to have the VB Script extract just the name entered by the visitor. In techno jargon, this called *parsing*. In this case, you must write instructions so that the VB Script engine extracts the name Natalie. Sounds like a major undertaking? Guess again, you already know how to do this.

Look at Example 12.8. This shows you a five-line VB Script that uses two functions presented early in the book. First, note that the value of the Name HTML control is assigned to the variable Visitor and that when we want the VB Script engine to reference the string returned by the control, we use the Visitor variable.

Example 12.8 Removing the Value from the String that is Returned by HTML

```
Dim MyForm, Visitor,intPos, strVal
Set MyForm = Document.CommentForm
Visitor = MyForm.Name.Value
intPos = InStr(Visitor, "=")
strVal = Mid(Visitor, intPos+1)
```

Next, the InStr() function is called. This function is told to look in the string referenced by the variable Visitor and find the position of the character =. The value returned by the InStr() function is 5. This means that the = character is the fifth character in the string Name=Natalie.

Why is this important to know? Because the value that we're looking for is in the next character position. Take a look at the last statement in this example and you'll see how this information is used to extract the information for which we're looking.

The VB Script calls the Mid() function. This function, as you recall, returns a portion of the string beginning with the character position that is specified in the argument. Remember, the variable Visitor represents the string Name=Natalie. The variable intPos contains an integer that represents the character position of the = character in the string.

We want the VB Script engine to begin copying characters of the string starting with the character that is to the right of the = character. In other words, begin copying from character position that is one more than the value of variable intPos. Therefore, Natalie is copied from the string Name=Natalie.

CONGRATULATIONS!

You have reached your goal of learning the VB Script language. Now you know how to combine the power of VB Script with HTML to create your own dramatic Web site. Be sure to keep this book near your computer when building your Web page. You'll find it easy to flip to the right section of the book if you run into a programming problem.

The remainder of the book is a quick reference guide. This is a perfect source for information at your finger tips.

Chapter 13

The VB Script Quick Reference

CONVERSION

Asc(string)

This function returns the ASCII character code value that corresponds to the first letter in a string. Caution: A run-time error will occur if the string contains no characters.

Example

```
Dim intAscVal
intAscVal = Asc("b")
```

CBool(expression)

Converts any valid expression into a variant of subtype Boolean. If the expression evaluates to 0, then a false is returned; otherwise, a true is returned. Caution: An expression that cannot be interpreted as a numeric value will cause a run-time error.

Example

```
Dim intVal
intVal = CBool(2-1)
```

CByte(expression)

Converts any valid expression into a variant of subtype Byte. It should be used to force byte arithmetic where currency, single-precision, double-precision, or integer arithmetic normally would occur. Use this function instead of Val() to ensure that the conversion reflects international differences, such as with decimal separators.

Example

```
Dim intVal
intVal = CByte(2-1)
```

CDate(date)

This function converts an expression into a date variant subtype. It recognizes date and time literals and numbers within the range of acceptable dates. Whole numbers are converted to a date. Fractional numbers are converted to a time of day, starting at midnight. This function recognizes date formats based on the date and time setting of your computer's system.

Example

```
Dim datDate
datDate = CDate("1/1/99")
```

CDbl(expression)

This function converts an expression to double-precision arithmetic. A double variable is a number ranging in value from –1.79769313486232E308 to –4.94065645841247E–324 for negative values and from 4.94065645841247E–324 to 1.79769313486232E308 for positive values. This gives greater accuracy than you would normally receive using the default subtype for currency or integer arithmetic. The function also provides international awareness when converting values to double precision, such as the different decimal and thousands separators used in various countries.

Example

```
Dim dblTotal
dblTotal = CDbl(9/5)
```

Chr(ASCIIcode)

This function returns a character associated with an ASCII code. The argument is the ASCII code for the character. In the following example, the function is passed the value 10, which converts to a carriage return; then it is passed a value 13, which is a line feed.

Example

```
MsgBox "First line" & Chr(13)+Chr(10) & "Second line.", 0
```

CInt(expression)

This function converts an expression to an integer subtype. An integer variable is a number ranging in value from –32,768 to 32,767. Only the integer portion of the expression is returned by the function. All decimal values are rounded up when the fractional part is 0.5 or above. A fractional part of 0.4 or below causes the value to be rounded down. It provides international awareness of thousands separators and decimal separators.

Example

```
Dim intTotal
intTotal = CInt(9/5)
```

CLng(expression)

This function converts an expression to a long subtype. A long variable is a number ranging in value from –2,147,483,648 to 2,147,483,647. It provides international awareness of thousands separators and decimal separators.

Example

```
Dim longTotal
longTotal = CLng(942*54.5)
```

CSng(expression)

This function converts an expression to a subtype single. A subtype single is also referred to as single-precision floating-point and can store values ranging from –3.402823E38 to –1.401298E-45 for negative values and from 1.401298E-45 to 3.402823E38 for positive values. It provides international awareness of thousands separators and decimal separators.

Example

```
Dim SingTotal
SingTotal = CSng(942/54.5)
```

CStr(expression)

This function converts an expression to a string subtype. The actual data returned depends on the expression, as shown in Table 13.1. It provides international awareness of thousands separators and decimal separators.

Example

```
Dim strInput
strInput = CStr(15)
```

Table 13.1 Return Values from the CStr() Function

If expression is	*CStr() returns a string containing*
Boolean	True or false
Date	A date in the short date format of your visitor's computer
Null	An error
Empty	A zero-length string
Error	The word *Error* followed by the error number
Other numeric	The number

Str(number)

This function converts a number to a string. The first space in the string is reserved for the sign of the number. A blank in the first space implies that the number is positive. Only the period is recognized as a valid decimal separator. If the international style is used within the number, then use the CStr() function to convert the number to a string.

Example

```
Dim strVal
strVal = Str(35)
```

Val(string)

This function returns the numbers contained in a string. The first character of the argument must be a character or a number; otherwise, an error occurs. It does not recognize dollar signs and commas, but does recognize radix prefixes, such as O for octal and H for hexadecimal. All blanks, tags, and line feeds are stripped from the argument.

Example

```
Dim intVal
intVal = Val("1235")
```

DATE AND TIME

Date()

This function returns the date on a visitor's computer, called the *system's date*.

Example

```
Dim datToday
datToday = Date()
```

DateSerial(year, month, day)

This function returns a date subtype for a specified year, month, and day. The year argument must be an integer in the range of 100 through 9999. The month must be an integer in the range of 1 through 12. The day must be an integer in the range of 1 through 31.

Example

```
Dim datDate
datDate = DateSerial(98,12,25)
```

DateValue(date)

This function returns a date subtype. The date argument is a string that represents a day from January 1, 100 through December 31, 9999. The date argument can also be any expression that represents date, time, or both date and time in the appropriate ranges. See TimeValue() for the proper ranges for time.

Example

```
Dim datDate
datDate = DateValue("12/25/98")
```

Day(date)

This function returns the day portion of a date. The day is an integer between 1 and 31, representing the day of the month.

Example

```
Dim datToday,intDay
datToday = Date()
intDay = Day(datToday)
```

Hour(time)

This function returns the hour portion of the time as a number between 0 and 23, inclusive, that represents the hour of the day.

Example

```
Dim tmNow, intHour
tmNow = Time()
intHour = Hour(tmNow)
```

Minute(time)

This function returns the minute portion of the time. The return value is a whole number between 0 and 59 and represents the minute of the hour.

Example

```
Dim intMinute
intMinute = Minute(Time())
```

Month(date)

This function returns the month portion of the date. The return value is a whole number between 1 and 12 that represents the month of the date.

Example

```
Dim intMonth
intMonth = Month(Date())
```

Now

Returns the current date and time from the system's clock on a visitor's computer.

Example

```
Dim datToday
datToday = Now()
```

Second(time)

This function returns the second portion of a time value, which is a whole number between 0 and 59 that represents the second of the minute.

Example

```
Dim intSecond
intSecond = Second(Time())
```

TimeSerial (hour, minute, second)

This function returns a date subtype that contains the time for a specific hour, minute, and second. The time is specified in three arguments. Each argument must contain an integer in the appropriate range for the portion of time. The hour must be between 0 and 23; the minute and second must be between 0 and 59.

Example

```
Dim tmTime
tmTime = TimeSerial(2,43,55)
```

TimeValue(time)

This function returns the date subtype that contains the time. The time argument is a string that represents time from 0:00:00 (12:00:00 AM) to 23:59:59 (11:59:59 PM). The time argument can also be any expression that represents the normal time range, which is 0 through 23 for hours and 0 through 59 for minutes and seconds.

Example

```
Dim tmTime
tmTime = TimeValue("22:23:45")
```

Weekday(date,[firstdayofweek])

This function returns a whole number that represents the day of the week. The date argument is a valid date subtype. The firstdayofweek argument is an integer that specifies which date of the week is the first day. If Sunday is the first day, then the firstdayofweek argument is optional. Table 13.2 contains values that are used to represent the day of the week both as the second argument and as the return value of the function.

Example

```
Dim intDay
intDay = Weekday("12/15/98")
```

Table 13.2 Values Used to Represent the Day of the Week

Value	*Description*
0	Use NLS API setting
1	Sunday
2	Monday
3	Tuesday
4	Wednesday
5	Thursday
6	Friday
7	Saturday

Year(date)

This function returns a whole number that represents the year of a valid date subtype.

Example

```
Dim intYear
intYear = Year("12/25/97")
```

DECISIONS

If then

```
If condition1 Then
    [statements]
[Else]
    [statements]
End If

If condition1 Then
    [statements]
[Else If condition2 Then]
    [statements]
[Else]
    [statements]
End If
```

This statement is used to execute one or more statements if a condition is true. The Else keyword can be used within the If Then statement to specify one or more statements that are executed if the condition is false. Another variation of the If Then statement uses the Else If keywords, which provide another condition that is tested if the first condition is false. If the second condition is true, the statements within the Else If keywords are executed. The Else and the Else If keywords are optional.

Example

```
If a = 35 Then
   MsgBox "Yes",0
Else
   MsgBox "No",0
End If
```

```
If a = 35 Then
    MsgBox "Yes",0
ElseIf a = 45 Then
    MsgBox "Almost",0
Else
    MsgBox "No",0
End If
```

Select Case

```
Select Case testexpression
Case expression
    [statements]
[Case expression]
    [statements]
[Else]
    [statements]
End Select
```

This statement executes one of many groups of statements depending on a test expression. The result of the test expression is compared with the expression of each Case statement. If a match occurs, then statements within the Case statement are executed and the Select Case statement terminates. If there is no match, then the statements following the Else statement are executed and the Select Case statement executes.

Example

```
Select Case A
Case 35
    MsgBox "Yes",0
Case 45
    MsgBox "Almost",0
Case Else
    MsgBox "No",0
End Select
```

INPUT AND OUTPUT

Input Box

```
InputBox(prompt[, title][, default][, xpos][, ypos][, helpfile,
context])
```

This function returns text entered by a visitor into a text box that is automatically displayed within a dialog box. The prompt argument contains the text on the screen that prompts a visitor to enter information into the text box. The title argument contains the text that appears on the title bar of the dialog box. The default argument contains the text that is entered into the text box as the default value when the dialog box is displayed. The xpos argument specifies, in twips, the horizontal distance of the left edge of the dialog box from the left edge of the screen. If this is omitted, the dialog box is horizontally centered. The ypos argument specifies, in twips, the vertical distance of the upper edge of the dialog box from the top of the screen. If this is omitted, the dialog box is vertically positioned approximately one-third of the way down the screen. The helfile argument contains the help file, if any, used when a visitor presses the Help button in the dialog box. The context argument contains the number of the help topic displayed when the help file is selected.

Example

```
Dim strName
strName = InputBox("Enter your name: ", "no name",35, 15,"myhelp file ",
"25")
```

Message Box

```
MsgBox prompt[, buttons][, title][, helpfile , context]
```

This statement causes a message to be displayed in a dialog box and waits for a visitor to select a button. The return value indicates which button was selected by a visitor (see Table 13.3). The prompt argument is the string that appears in the message box. The button argument is an integer value that represents the sum of the button values for the variety of buttons that are to be displayed in the dialog box (see Table 13.4). The title argument is the string that appears on the title bar of the dialog box. The helpfile argument is the name of the help file that assists a visitor to understand the message. The context argument is the number of the topic that is to be displayed when the help file is accessed by the function. All arguments except the prompt argument are optional.

Example

```
MsgBox "Hello!",0,"Welcome Message","myhelpfile ","35"
```

Table 13.3 Return Value from the MsgBox() Function

Value	*Button Chosen*
1	OK
2	Cancel
3	Abort
4	Retry
5	Ignore
6	Yes
7	No

Table 13.4 Values for the Button Argument

Value	*Description*
0	Display OK button only
1	Display OK and Cancel buttons
2	Display Abort, Retry, and Ignore buttons
3	Display Yes, No, and Cancel buttons

(Continued)

Table 13.4 (Continued)

4	Display Yes and No buttons
5	Display Retry and Cancel buttons
6	Display CriticalMessage icon
32	Display Warning Query icon
48	Display WarningMessage icon
64	Display Information Message icon
0	First button is default
256	Second button is default
512	Third button is default
768	Fourth button is default
0	Application modal: the user must respond to the message box before continuing work in the current application
4096	System modal: all applications are suspended until the user responds to the message box

LOOPS

Do While and Do Until

```
Do [{While | Until} condition]
    [statements]
    [Exit Do]
    [statements]
Loop
```

This statement continues to execute a series of statements contained within the loop as long as the condition expression is true or false. The Do

While loop executes statements if the condition statement is true. The Do Until loop executes statements until the condition statement is true. The Do loop can be terminated before the condition is met by placing the Exit Do statement within the Do loop. There can be a condition in which the statements within the Do loop are never evaluated by the VB Script engine.

Example

```
Do While strName = "Bob Smith"
    MsgBox "Hello, Bob!",0
Loop
Do Until intVal = 20
    intVal = intVal + 1
Loop
```

Do Loop While and Do Loop Until

```
Do
    [statements]
    [Exit Do]
    [statements]
Loop[{While | Until} condition]
```

This statement continues to execute statements within the Do loop as long as the condition is either true or false. The Do Loop While executes statements while the condition is true. The Do Loop Until executes statements until the condition is true. In all cases, statements within the Do loop are evaluated at least once.

Example

```
Do
    MsgBox("Hello, Bob!",0)
```

```
Loop While strName = "Bob Smith"
Do
   intVal = intVal + 1
Loop Until intVal = 20
```

Counter Loop

```
For counter = start To end [Step stepval]
    [statements]
    [Exit For]
    [statements]
Next
```

This statement executes statements between the For and Next keywords a specific number of times. The counter is the variable that is assigned a value that is incremented each revolution of the loop. The start value represents the beginning value assigned to the counter variable. This value is incremented. The end value is the maximum number of revolutions of the loop. The loop is incremented sequentially unless the Step keyword is used. The stepval value is the interval that is skipped each revolution of the loop. If the start value is 1 and the end value is 10, there will be 10 revolutions of the loop; however, if the stepval is 2, then there will be 5 revolutions of the loop. The first revolution is 1, the second revolution is 3, and so forth. The Exit For statement terminates the loop before the maximum number of revolutions is reached.

Example

```
For a = 1 To 10 Step 2
    MsgBox "This is number " & a,0
Next
```

While Loop

```
While condition
[statements]
Wend
```

The While loop executes statements within the loop as long as the condition is true. Microsoft recommends that the Do While loop be used in place of the While loop.

Example

```
While a = 35
    MsgBox "Hello world.",0
Wend
```

MATHEMATICS

Abs(number)

This function returns the absolute value of a number, regardless of sign, where the number can be a numeric expression. A 0 is returned if the variable is uninitialized.

Example

```
Dim intNum, intABS
intNum = -4
intABS = Abs(intNum)
```

Atn(number)

This function returns the arc tangent of any valid numeric expression.

Example

```
Dim intVal
intVal = Atn(30)
```

Cos(number)

This function returns the cosine of the argument number, which is the ratio of two sides of a right triangle determined by dividing the side adjacent to the angle by the length of the hypotenuse. The argument to this function is a numeric expression that describes an angle in radians. Hint: To convert the radians to degrees, multiply radians by $180/\pi$; to convert degrees to radians, multiply degrees by $\pi/180$.

Example

```
Dim intVal
intVal = Cos(30)
```

Exp(number)

This function returns the base of a natural logarithm raised to a power and complements the action of the Log() function. Caution: An error occurs when the number is greater than 709.782712893.

Example

```
MsgBox Exp(25),0
```

Fix(number)

This function returns the integer portion of a number. If the number argument is negative, then the function returns the first negative integer greater than or equal to that number. In the following example, the –7.4 is converted to –7.

Example

```
Dim intVal
intVal = Fix(-7.4)
```

Hex(number)

This function returns a string that represents the hexadecimal value of a number. The number should be a whole number; however, the Hex() function automatically rounds the fraction of the number to the next whole number. Hexadecimal numbers can be represented by preceding the number with H. For example, H10 is the hexadecimal format for 16.

Example

```
MsgBox Hex(15),0
```

Int(number)

This function returns the integer portion of a number. If the number argument is negative, then the function returns the first negative integer less than or equal to that number. In this example, the –7.4 is converted to –8.

Example

```
Dim intVal
intVal = Int(-7.4)
```

Log(number)

This function returns the log of a number or any valid numeric expression that is greater than 0.

Example

```
Dim Val
Val = Log(45)
```

Oct(number)

This function returns a string that contains the octal value of a number. If not a whole number, the number is rounded to the nearest whole number before being converted to an octal value. An octal number can be directly represented by using the O notation before the number; for example, O10 is the octal notation for the decimal 8.

Example

```
Dim strOctalValue
strOctalValue = Oct(15)
```

Randomize[number]

This statement initializes the Rnd() function by giving it a new seed value. The number argument is the seed value. If the number argument is omitted, then the system timer is used as the new seed value.

Example

```
Dim intVal
Randomize
intVal = Rnd()* 100
```

Rnd[(number)]

This function returns a random number of less than 1 but greater than or equal to 0. The number argument, called the *seed* and optional, determines how the random number will be generated (see Table 13.5).

Caution: For any given initial seed, the same number sequence is generated because each successive call to the function uses the previous number as a seed for the next number in the sequence. Before calling the function, use the Randomize statement without an argument to initialize the random-number generator with a seed based on the system timer.

Example

```
Dim intNum
Randomize
intNum = 100 * Rnd()
```

Table 13.5 Number Arguments for the Rnd() Function

If number is	*Rnd generates*
Less than 0	The same number every time, using number as the seed
Greater than 0	The next random number in the sequence
Equal to 0	The most recently generated number
Not supplied	The next random number in the sequence

Sgn(number)

This function returns an integer that indicates the sign of the expression. A value of 1 is returned if the expression is greater than 0; a value of 0 is returned if the expression is equal to 0; and a value of –1 is returned if the expression is less than 0.

Example

```
Dim intVal
intVal = Sgn(-5)
```

Sin(number)

This function returns the sine of the argument number, which is an angle stated in radians. The sine is the ratio of two sides of a right triangle, determined by dividing the length of the side opposite the angle by the length of the hypotenuse.

Example

```
Dim sgnVal
sgnVal = Sin(30)
```

Sqr(number)

This function returns the square root of the argument number. The argument must be equal to or greater than 0.

Example

```
Dim sqrVal
sqrVal = Sqr(5)
```

Tan(number)

This function returns the tangent of an angle expressed in radians. The tangent is the ratio of two sides of a right triangle. The ratio is determined by dividing the length of the side opposite the angle by the length of the side adjacent to the angle.

Example

```
Dim intVal
intVal = Tan(30)
```

PROCEDURES

Call name (argumentlist)

This function transfers control of the VB Script to a procedure or a function procedure. The name is the name of the procedure or function procedure. The argument list is the arguments that are required by the procedure or function procedure. Each argument in the argument list must be separated by a comma. Caution: You can eliminate the keyword Call and just use the name of the procedure or function procedure. However, if you do, you must also eliminate the parentheses around the argument list.

Example

```
Call ReadName("First")
```

FUNCTIONS

```
Function name(arglist]
    [statements]
    [name=expression]
    [Exit Function]
```

```
    [statements]
    [name=expression]
End Function
```

A function is a function procedure that contains one or more statements executed by the VB Script engine when the VB Script calls the function procedure. Name is the name of the function, and arglist is a list of arguments passed to the function by the VB Script when the function is called. Statements are any valid VB Script statement. A function can return a value to the calling statement in the VB Script by assigning that value to the name of the function. A function can be terminated before the End Function statement is reached by using the Exit Function statement. Statements that follow the Exit Function statement are not evaluated by the VB Script engine.

Example

```
Static Function TotalComp(intSalary, intBonus)
    TotalComp = intSalary + intBonus
End Function

Dim intTotalPay
intTotalPay = TotalComp(20000,1500)
```

Rem

This statement causes the VB Script engine to ignore the line in the VB Script. Any characters that follow the Rem statement on the line can be used as comments within the VB Script. An apostrophe (') is an allowable alternative to Rem, and makes the comments a little more readable.

Example

```
Rem Display a message box
MsgBox "Hello, world.",0
```

SUBPROCEDURES

```
Subname(arglist)
[statements]
[Exit Sub]
[statements]
End Sub
```

This statement creates a subprocedure that can be called by a VB Script. Subname is the name of the subprocedure. The arglist represents arguments that are passed to the subprocedure. The statements are VB Script language statements evaluated by the VB Script engine when the subprocedure is called by the VB Script. The Exit Sub statement is used to exit the subprocedure before all the statements in the subprocedure are evaluated by the VB Script engine. The End Sub keywords specify the end of the subprocedure. Each time a subprocedure terminates, values assigned to variables within the subprocedure are erased.

Example

```
CalculateComp( intSalary, intBonus)
   MsgBox "Compensation is: " & intSalary + intBonus, 0
End Sub
```

On Error Resume Next

This statement directs the VB Script engine to continue to evaluate the VB Script even if an error is detected. Without this statement, the VB Script engine stops evaluating the VB Script whenever an error occurs and displays an error message. When an error is detected, the VB Script engine jumps to the statement immediately following the statement that caused the error.

Example

```
On Error Resume Next
If a = 35 Then
    MsgBox "Yes",0
Else
    MsgBox "No",0
End If
```

STRINGS

InStr([start,]string1, string2[, compare])

This function returns the position of the first occurrence of a string within another string. The start argument is the numeric expression that determines the starting character for the search. The function starts with the first character by default. The string1 argument is the string that is to be searched. The string2 argument is the string being searched for in string1. The compare argument is a numeric value that specifies the kind of search to be conducted. A value of 0 indicates a binary comparison (default) and a value of 1 indicates a textual comparison that is case insensitive.

Example

```
Dim intPos

intPos = InStr("Bob Smith", "Smith")
```

LCase(string)

This function converts all the letters in a string to lowercase.

Example

```
Dim strLower
strLower = LCase("Bob Smith")
```

Left(string, length)

This function returns a specific number of characters, beginning with the first character of the string. The string argument is the string to be searched. The length argument is the integer value that specifies the maximum number of characters to be returned. In the following example, the function returns the letters B-o-b.

Example

```
Dim strPart
strPart = Left("Bob Smith",3)
```

Len(string)

This function returns the number of characters in a string.

Example

```
Dim intVal
intVal = Len("Bob Smith")
```

LTrim(string)

This function removes leading spaces from a string.

Example

```
Dim strTrimmed
strTrimmed = LTrim("     Bob")
```

Mid(string, start[, length])

This function returns a specific number of characters from a string, beginning with a specified character position in the string. The string argument is the string to be searched. The start argument is the integer of the character position where the function begins copying characters. The length argument is the integer that specifies the number of characters to be copied. The following example returns the characters S-m-i-t-h.

Example

```
Dim strName
strName = Mid("Bob Smith",5,5)
```

RTrim(string)

This function removes trailing spaces from a string.

Example

```
Dim strName
strName = RTrim("Bob     ")
```

Right(string, length)

This function returns a specific number of characters, beginning with the rightmost character of the string. The string argument is the string to be searched. The length argument is the integer value that specifies the maximum number of characters that are to be returned. In the following example, the function returns the letters S-m-i-t-h.

Example

```
Dim strPart
strPart = Right("Bob Smith",5)
```

StrComp(string1, string2[, compare])

This function shows the result of a string comparison. A return value of 0 means that the strings are the same. A return value of –1 means that string1 is less than string2. A return value of 1 means that string1 is greater than string2. The arguments string1 and string2 are the two strings being compared. The third argument is an integer that specifies the type of string comparison. A value of 0 indicates a binary comparison (default) and a value of 1 indicates a textual comparison that is case insensitive.

Example

```
Dim strFirstName, strLastName
strFirstName = "Bob"
strLastName = "Smith"
If StrComp(string1, string2[, compare])
    MsgBox "Is an OLE Automation object."
Else
    MsgBox "Is not an OLE Automation object."
End if
```

String(number, character)

This function returns a string that contains a repeated character. The number argument specifies the number of times the character is repeated, also known as the string's *length*. The character argument is the character to be repeated in the string. The character argument can be a string. If so, then only the first character of the string argument is repeated. If the number argument does not contain a valid number, then NULL is returned.

Example

```
Dim strMyStr
strMyStr = String(10,"B")
```

Ucase(string)

This converts all the characters in a string to uppercase.

Example

```
Dim strUCase
strUCase = Ucase("bob smith")
```

VARIABLES

Dim varname[([subscripts])][, varname[([subscripts])]]...

This statement is used to define a variable or an array variable. The varname is the name of the variable or the array variable. The subscript is used to dimension an array variable; up to 60 multiple dimensions can be declared. The subscript always contains the upper dimension of an array variable. The first element of an array variable is identified as 0. All variables and array variables defined at the VB Script level are available to all procedures within the VB Script. All variables and array variables defined at the procedural level are available to that procedure. This statement is used to declare a dynamic array variable by excluding an upper boundary dimension within the parentheses. No value is placed within the parentheses. The ReDim statement must be used to change the dimension of a dynamic array variable.

Example

```
Dim intTotal, intSalary(10), intBonus()
ReDim intBonus(10)
```

Erase arraylist

This statement erases an array variable. If the array variable is of a fixed size (not a dynamic array variable), then all elements of the array are set to 0 but the memory used by the array variable is not freed. If the array variable is a dynamic array variable, then memory used by the dynamic array variable is freed. A dynamic array variable that is erased must be redeclared using the ReDim statement before the dynamic array variable can be used again.

Example

```
Dim intSalary(10), intBonus()
ReDim intBonus(10)
Erase intSalary(), intBonus()
ReDim intBonus(10)
```

IsDate(expression)

This function returns a true or false value indicating whether an expression can be converted to a date. A value of 0 is returned if the expression cannot be converted to a date; otherwise, a value of 1 is returned by the function. The ranges vary among operating systems. In Microsoft Windows, the range of valid dates is January 1, 100 AD through December 31, 9999 AD.

Example

```
Dim strBirthDate
strBirthDate = "12/25/95"
If IsDate(strBirthDate) Then
   MsgBox "Can convert."
Else
   MsgBox "Cannot convert."
End if
```

IsEmpty(expression)

This function returns a true or false value indicating whether an expression was initialized. A value of 0 is returned if the expression is not initialized; otherwise, a value of 1 is returned by the function. The expression argument is most often a single name variable.

Example

```
Dim strBirthDate
strBirthDate = "12/25/95"
If IsEmpty(strBirthDate) Then
   MsgBox "Is initialized."
Else
   MsgBox "Is not initialized."
End if
```

IsNull(expression)

This function returns a true or false value indicating that an expression has no valid data or has a NULL value. A value of 0 is returned if the expression does not have a NULL value; otherwise, a value of 1 is returned by the function.

Example

```
Dim strBirthDate
strBirthDate = "12/25/95"
If IsNull(strBirthDate)Then
   MsgBox "Data is null."
Else
   MsgBox "Data is not null."
End if
```

IsNumeric(expression)

This function returns a Boolean value that indicates whether an expression can be evaluated as a number. A false is returned if the expression cannot be evaluated as a number; otherwise, a true is returned.

Example

```
Dim intVal
intVal = 1234
If IsNumber(intVal)Then
   MsgBox "Can convert."
Else
   MsgBox "Cannot convert."
End if
```

[Let] varname=expression

This statement assigns a value of an expression to a variable. The Let keyword is optional.

Example

```
Dim strName
Let strName = "Bob Smith"
```

ReDim[Preserve] varname(subscripts [, varname(subscripts] ...

This statement redimensions an array variable. Preserve is a keyword that instructs the VB Script engine to retain the values assigned to the elements of the array variable while the array variable is redimensioned. The varname argument is the name of the array variable, and the subscript argument is the new dimension of the array variable.

Example

```
Dim Emp
ReDim Emp(12)
```

UBound(arrayname[, dimension])

This function returns the largest subscript for the dimension specified in the second argument of the array specified in the first argument. If the array has one dimension, then the dimension argument is optional.

Example

```
Dim EmpNum(30,5), intUpper
intUpper = UBound(EmpNum, 2)
```

VarType(varname)

This function shows the subtype of a variable. Table 13.6 contains the return values of this function.

Example

```
dim intVal, intType
intVal = 345.23
intType = VarType(intVal)
```

Table 13.6 Return Values of the VarType() Function

Value	*Variable Type Description*
0	Empty (uninitialized)
1	Null (no valid data)
2	Integer
3	Long integer
4	Single-precision floating-point number
5	Double-precision floating-point number
6	Currency
7	Date
8	String
9	OLE automation object
10	Error
11	Boolean
12	Variant (used only with arrays of variants)
13	Non-OLE automation object
17	Byte
8192	Array

Index